AMERICAN CASTLES

Julian Cavalier

SOUTH BRUNSWICK AND NEW YORK:
A. S. BARNES AND COMPANY
LONDON: THOMAS YOSELOFF LTD

© 1973 by A. S. Barnes and Co., Inc.

A. S. Barnes and Co., Inc.
Cranbury, New Jersey 08512

Thomas Yoseloff Ltd
108 New Bond Street
London W1Y OQX, England

Library of Congress Cataloging in Publication Data

Cavalier, Julian, 1931–
      American castles.

      1. Castles—United States.   I.   Title.
NA705.C39   917.3′03   72-6394
ISBN 0-498-01254-9

To
my parents and family
whose understanding and encouragement helped me
through the completion of this manuscript

CONTENTS

PREFACE

The following pages illustrate and attempt to describe the brief history of some of the more prominent and unusual castle structures that are found throughout the United States. With few exceptions, the majority of these castellated structures were constructed between the latter part of the last century and the early part of the present. Each of these structures displays its own style of architecture, a representative reflection in many instances of the dreams and motivations of men who sought to build with attitudes and judgments that understandably varied considerably with the individual and the age.

Some of the American castles were adapted from designs and memorial reminiscence of European chateaux and castles, while others are individually unique in castle architectural style and design. In many instances the castle are replete with furniture and vast treasures gathered from worldwide sources. Others, though less elaborate in detail and furnishings, are meticulously well adapted for their styles and personal tastes of the builder. Though the overall designs vary considerably, from vast and lavish architectural masterpieces to grand simplicity of individual temperament and effort, their character as castle architecture is not lacking in either case. Some of these magnificent structures are only shells of their former days and several are no longer existing. The razing of such structures will undoubtedly leave little with which future generations can associate in regard to this style of architecture, already becoming scarce in America.

Compared to their monumental European counterparts, whose existence has simmered in the centuries of time, the American castles, though fewer in number, do have their reasons for being here. Their existence grew from a compulsion of the builder to create a structure of significance, either in the grand manner or in individual expression. Each of the castles has its own beauty of form and history as different from one another as their architectural design, but with the common bond of creation linking them together. Not only in such a link does this bond entirely lie, but also in the vitality of form, imagination, and an elegance that refuses to die.

Taken together, the castles pictured here present one aspect of architectural development in America that is relatively unheard of beyond its borders. One rarely thinks of America in terms of castles, and yet here they stand, almost as a protest against the ugliness of an industrial age, proudly displaying their grandeur of days gone by and wholly representative of the best that their owner's means and taste afforded. Though relatively short in their existence, it is hoped that the remaining castles still standing will last long enough to become a part of America's heritage and not succumb to the present era of the bulldozer and blitzkrieg architecture.

ACKNOWLEDGMENTS

I wish to express my sincerest appreciation and grateful thanks to many individuals, historians, curators, historical societies, museums, and numerous other institutions and libraries for their attention, courtesy, and assistance to me when gathering material for this book.

Special thanks to: Jan Blair, Harry D. Andrews, Lennart Palme, Tara Stoke, Ray Lydston, Tania Zahediakin, Corinne Witham, Louisa M. Talbot, Hazel Simpson, Mary H. Biondi, Sisters of the Carmelite Monastery, Hortense Lunsford, Motherhouse of the Sisters of Mercy, Windham, N.H., Alys Freeze, Virginia Daiker, F. W. Van Name, Gabrielle Apone, Judith Topaz, Anne Brunsell.

Also to:

The Chicago Historical Society

Hammond Museum, Incorporated, Gloucester, Massachusetts

Passaic County Historical Society, Paterson, N.J.

U.S. Library of Congress, Washington, D.C.

Watertown Daily Times, Watertown, N.Y.

State of New York Department of Commerce

Treadway Thousand Islands Club, N.Y.

Virginia Museum of Fine Arts

State of Connecticut Park & Forest Commission

Metropolitan Museum of Art, N.Y.

National Trust for Historic Preservation, Washington, D.C.

Virginia State Library

Previews, Incorporated, N.Y.

Louisiana State Library

Chatham Public Library, N.J.

B. H. Bartel Library, Freeport, Maine

Denver Public Library

State Historical Society of Wisconsin

University of Kentucky Libraries

Tennessee State Library & Archives

Franklin County Library, Winchester, Tennessee

Brownsville Historical Society, Brownsville, Pennsylvania

Beaver College, Glenside, Pennsylvania

University of Georgia Libraries

Chamber of Commerce, Cooperstown, N.Y.

New York State Historical Association

The Western Reserve Historical Society, Cleveland, Ohio

State of Mississippi Department of Archives & History

State of California, Department of Parks and Recreation

Union Pacific Railroad Company

The Atchison, Topeka and Santa Fe Railway Company

South Lake Tahoe News Bureau

AMERICAN CASTLES

] 1 [

HAMMOND CASTLE

NEAR THE LOVELY NEW ENGLAND COASTAL TOWN of Gloucester, Massachusetts, and located high above the pounding surf on the rocky cliffs overlooking the Reef of Norman's Woe, stands an imposing, medieval castle, complete with turrets, battlements, and drawbridge. This castle was constructed between 1925 and 1928 by inventor John Hays Hammond, Jr., whose plans of the castle incorporated much ancient architecture and treasures of the Old World. Hammond was a very prolific inventor for more than seventy years, holding nearly a thousand patents, many of which contribute to our daily lives and national security.

Hammond was born in San Francisco on April 13, 1888. His father, John Hays Hammond, was a famous geologist and mining engineer who traveled the globe to wherever his work took him. He was also employed as chief mining engineer for the Guggenheim mining family at a tax-free million dollars a year salary. In 1911 he represented the United States as special ambassador at the coronation of King George V of England. Included among the family's friends were such distinguished persons as Alexander Graham Bell, Marchese Gugielmo Marconi, Thomas Edison, Nikola Tesla, and the Wright brothers. John Hammond, Jr.'s uncle, John Hays, was also widely known in his day as one of the founders of the famous Texas Rangers. During an interview John Hammond, Jr. recalled, "As an engineer, I would be second best to my father, and as a

man of action, I could never hope to compete with my uncle. But I had a compulsion to compete with both of them. I wasn't going to waste my life clipping stock coupons." Traveling widely with his parents, living wherever his father's work took them, young John Hammond spent much of his early life in England, Washington, and Gloucester, Massachusetts.

At an early age John Hammond, Jr. began to develop and demonstrate his talent of inventiveness. He received his preparatory education at Lawrenceville School in New Jersey. While there, he constructed one of his first inventions, a circuit breaker, which he cleverly installed on the door of his room so as to overcome the nightly "lights out" rule of the school. Upon graduating from this school he continued his education by entering the Sheffield Scientific School of Yale University, where he distinguished himself in scientific studies, receiving a bachelor of science degree upon graduating in 1910. He also distinguished himself at Yale by spacing railroad torpedoes on tracks of the New Haven as a new means of celebrating a football victory. The arrangement of the torpedoes boomed out around the countryside to the rhythm of "Boola-boola" as the midnight express roared by from Boston. In Washington, D.C. he took a job in the Patent Office as a clerk, where he stayed for two years to become an authority on the patents of radio and telephony. It was during this period that young John Hammond was excited about the possibilities of remote control by radio, a field he was convinced was wide open to him.

The Hammond Radio Research Laboratory was soon established by the twenty-four-year-old Hammond with the support of his father, who was able and willing to aid him with the costly equipment for his experiments. Included among the equipment were high-voltage generators and alternators that astonished his father as they noisily turned over and cast off bright blue sparks, resembling something of a Frankenstein laboratory. "Your uncle and I have faced sudden death before," his father said, "but this looks too sudden." The "few dollars" his father did not mind risking for the laboratory and equipment turned out to be a quarter of a million. But the experiments proved fruitful, and frightening to the bewildered fishermen of Gloucester Bay who watched in amazement as a crewless boat moved by invisible force about the bay. Excited by his success of controlling the boat by remote radio control, young Hammond forgot about the controls, running into the house to tell his father, while the boat sped across the water, dashing itself against the rocky shore. Another similar experiment was later conducted with the addition of a gyroscope installed in another boat also radio controlled with great success. In a later experiment Hammond succeeded in sending a yacht 120 miles from Gloucester to Boston and having it return by remote control. The Navy captain on board stated that it was "like riding a ghost ship." Thus, in 1914, just prior to the Great War, the basis of all radio control was successfully established by John Hays Hammond, Jr. Hammond's "electric dog" invention, controlled with selenium-cell eyes following a beam of light, caused a great sensation at the time it was used on a vaudeville tour. But this invention proved more than just a novelty as it brought closer the development of radar.

The work continued with experiments, and many successful developments followed resulting in over 150 patents that were of military value by 1916. Among these experiments was Hammond's development of radio torpedoes and a system for preventing the enemy from jamming military orders given by radio. The War Department had asked Congress to pay Hammond three quarters of a million dollars for the use of his patents. Though the appropriation was approved by the House, the Senate failed to do so until 1932, when he finally received payment after sixteen years had passed.

Another more serious situation with the government occurred during the First World War. In 1914 Hammond had invented a light, incendiary bomb that neither the American nor British governments were interested in buying. When such bombs began to fall on London, Hammond was accused of having sold out to the Germans. But he was fully cleared of the charge after one of his former employees was caught spying in Washington and confessed to stealing the plans for the bomb. "After that, Washington became more security conscious and I was able to persuade them that patent applications covering instruments of war should not be filed in the general patent office for all to see."

Hammond's contributions to numerous scientific developments include radar, telephone amplification, the radio tube, and many other important inventions, including some of the earliest experiments in frequency modulation broadcasting in addition to private communications systems. In 1919 the George Washington University awarded him an honorary doctor of science degree, and in 1923 the Radio Corporation of America bought his patents in the field of radio. His contributions were fundamental discoveries perhaps appreciated more by specialists and by others who used them as a basis for further developments and inventions. Hammond was greatly interested in the arts, especially music, where additional inventions were further developed with the advice of such prominent friends as Leopold Stokowski and Serge Koussevitzky.

In the early 1920s, shortly after Mussolini seized power in Italy, Hammond was on a pleasure trip in Rome where he was surprised to receive a midnight call from Il Duce's office requesting to see him the next day. The purpose of the visit became known to the puzzled Hammond when Mussolini revealed that he wanted a foolproof secret radio communications system. The reluctant Hammond cautiously replied that the system would take a year to set up, and much of the elaborate and scarce equipment was hard to get. But Mussolini's efficiency was proved by delivering of the equipment several days before schedule. Hammond became very discouraged when he later learned that the communications system had been used to trap anti-Fascists, some of whom had been Hammond's personal friends. During World War II Hammond developed numerous projects for United States national defense and continued to work on secret projects for the government up until the time of his death.

Though Hammond produced numerous ingenious inventions during his lifetime that would place him among the great inventors of the world, he remained generally unknown to the public. This was perhaps due to his work being under the secrecy imposed by the government, and the public heard nothing of it. Much of his work was a basic foundation upon which other inventors could benefit. Not being one for publicity, he preferred the seclusion of his daily life to do what he wanted to do and enjoy every moment of it.

Prior to his entry into college, Hammond spent many years in Europe, where his youthful interest in the arts were further developed by his travels in the Old World. In later years he made trips to Europe, where he was able to obtain many fine art objects for his private collection by using his own ship to explore the many places where such objects of art were still to be found.

Based on Hammond's own plans, a castle museum was soon to be erected that would house and exhibit the valuable and growing collection, in addition to providing laboratory space for electronic research. A suitable, isolated site was chosen, free from electrical interference, in a wooded area in Gloucester, Massachusetts. In 1925 the construction began on a large, masonry castle that was to be dedicated to the arts and sciences, at a cost of untold millions.

The structure was planned in three major parts, the northern portion of which was to be occupied by laboratories and offices in a small, two-story, modern wing. The remainder of the structure is distinctly of an early period of architecture, with the central portion consisting of twelfth-century fortified towers and the fourteenth-century Great Hall. Living quarters of the fifteenth century castle architecture found in France and Italy make up the southern portion of the structure. The castle was named *Abbadia Mare,* Abbey by the Sea, by Hammond, who incorporated into the castle actual portions of ancient dwellings of Old-World architectural beauty and design.

In addition to the northern wing and Great Hall, plans called for a reception hall, an entrance and lower hall, a chapel section with a living or reading room, a refectory, the Gothic Room, the Sicilian Room, museum galleries on three floors, the Princess Zalessky Room, roof gardens, a terrace room, and a courtyard with a Roman pool. Housed within this blending of various styles and period architecture are rare, priceless art treasures rich in beauty and antiquity.

An ancient gangway from a ruined wharf was secured by Hammond, who was unable to find an old castle drawbridge during his journeys to Europe. By his ingenuity he converted the wharf into the drawbridge that now leads to the castle's front door. Heavy chains secured high up on the stone walls lead down and are anchored to the front ends of the drawbridge, which at this point are flanked on either side by fierce-looking lion figures sculptured in stone. The heavily constructed and protective drawbridge door contains a small, crossbar-protected window opening, typically used in such castle doors to inspect approaching visitors prior to their gaining entrance.

The reception hall contains such treasures as the second-century Roman stone-plaque eagle and whale, sixteenth-century German wood carving of Saint Matthew, a carved, oak, Sardinian bench of the same period, and other objects and furniture from the fifteenth to the eighteenth centuries.

The entrance hall displays, among other ancient pieces, a fifteenth-century Russian icon of Saint Dionysius, who, in the fourth century, was missionary to Gaul. From Germany a very heavy seventeenth-century church treasure chest is located here, and resting on a mantle is a fifteenth-century Italian bronze lion candlestick. Set in the wall of this chamber are pieces of coral masonry brought from the ruins of the first church built by Columbus in the New World at Santo Domingo. Hammond recovered other Columbian relics from Santo Domingo that can been seen in the first-floor gallery.

A railing is carved into the stone wall of the newell staircase that leads down into the lower hall, where objects and furniture from the thirteenth century are found. A well-detailed marble tombstone of the second century is also located here in addition to an ornately carved fifteenth-century Gothic dowry chest, a valued possession in the Middle ages. A thirteenth-century Russian icon rests over the door of the Great Hall.

The Great Hall is a long, high room beautifully designed in stone with wood arches spanning the upper portions of the sixty-foot-high ceiling. Within the hundred-foot length of this hall are several interesting alcoves, each with their splendid Gothic entrances that open to the treasures they contain. Deep, encased windows are located high upon the upper portions of the side walls, and three stained-glass windows can also be seen from within this hall. One of these windows is a large, beautifully detailed rose window reproduced and patterned similar to the rose window of the ancient Rheims Cathedral in France. Built into the side of one wall is a thirteenth-century fireplace that Hammond secured from the ruins of a castle in France. Opposite this fireplace is an exquisite fifteenth-century gilded wood carving that surrounds the famous organ console built by Hammond.

The magnificent pipe organ that Hammond built over a period of twenty years is in an eighty-five-foot-high stone tower with the organ console open to the great hall. (This Hammond instrument is not to be confused with those of W. K. Hammond, who is of no relation.) This spectacular instrument has over ten thousand pipes, four manuals, 144 stops, and a floating baroque section.

Located within one of the Gothic arched sleeves is an intricately designed and inlaid treasure chest of Oriental origin, but brought by the Moors into Spain. Another arched alcove contains a sixteenth-century eagle lectern. At one end of the Great Hall is the fifteenth-century bishop's stall with an elaborately carved, high back. A unique and beautifully crafted furnishing is the German Gothic credence of the fifteenth century with carved hunting scenes in black oak and finished in wrought-iron trim.

A small but interesting chamber called the Chapel was used by Hammond as a small living or reading room. In addition to several ancient relics and furnishings, this room also contains a thirteenth-century fireplace over which is placed, in carved relief, a Madonna and Child, also made in the same period. Numerous masterpieces of art objects and furnishings fill this noble hall whose Gothic interior appealingly sets the background and mood for their display.

The Great Hall opens into a secluded courtyard where several ages are represented, spanning many centuries within its confines. The walls of the courtyard are partially made up of the sides and end portions of actual houses that were brought in from abroad and joined together, forming a charming, quiet area similar to the open squares found in an-

cient towns. Green shrubs and trees gracefully border the centrally located pool, which adds an atmosphere of coolness and shade to the quaintness of this lovely courtyard. Flowers also border this pool of Roman construction, as do fifteenth-century columns, which are spaced along the thirty-foot length of its sides. At one end of the pool is a building entry doorway above which is mounted a twelfth-century wooden Christ from Italy. The opposite end contains a statue set beneath an arched niche spanning the width of the pool. Flagstone paths surround the pool and border the various portions of the walls and ancient building facades that enclose the courtyard.

The house facade from Amiens is dated about 1470 and shows carved details of a merchant's activities. The interesting bottle-glass windows are patterned in Byzantine grapevine trim of the fifteenth century. Another interesting house facade viewed from the courtyard is from Tours, and is of the French Crusades period. Its old, slate roof gracefully shelters its patterned timber and brick construction and thirteenth-century carved wood frieze, which pictures a medieval circus.

The courtyard also exhibits a fireplace made from a sixth-century altar, a mounted thirteenth-century Italian monastery bell, and a tomb of a pre-Christian child. Hammond found this tomb, which is believed to have been made about 200 B.C., in an old, Roman wall located near the Forum. Several other interesting objects are also displayed about the courtyard, which is equipped with facilities for producing artificial rain of varying intensities ranging from light sprinkles to heavy downpours, in addition to creating the effects of moonlight and realistic sunlight.

From the courtyard a column-supported, arched bridge leads to the Gothic room, an ancient bedchamber with original furniture. Most interesting in this room are the floor tiles, which were brought from the palace of the son of Christopher Columbus. Bottle-glass window inserts show an interesting design as does the Romanesque chandelier holding candlecups. Several ancient pieces of fine-detailed furniture are placed about the room, and of particular interest is the fourteenth-century Italian wrought-iron bed with silk canopy interwoven in patterns with gold.

The refectory is wood-paneled with a Gothic patterned tile floor containing several original thirteenth-century French tiles. The wood-paneled ceiling is fifteenth-century Spanish with small, suspended, Spanish wrought-iron lanterns of the fourteenth century. The Italian fifteenth-century walnut table is accompanied by metal-studded and leather-upholstered Spanish-Italian chairs. In addition to several other ancient objects is the thirteenth-century ecclesiastical, two-section panel painting with an intricately carved frame enclosing the scenes of the torture and burial of Saint Romanus.

Adjoining the refectory is the Sicilian Room, a small chamber with a Sardinian door, one side of which is carved and the other iron plated. Several interesting ceramic tile designs are found here in addition to ancient pottery and cooking utensils.

The museum galleries, which occupy three floors, contain numerous ancient art objects, tapestries, and furniture in addition to ancient, built-in architecture, such as the eighth-century marble doorway on the second floor. These galleries with their contents are best appreciated by viewing them in their arranged settings. The first and second floors display beautifully designed and ancient tapestries from the fourteenth, fifteenth, and sixteenth centuries, many of which are from France. A sarcophagus of the first century, from Rome, and a seventeenth-century court cupboard from Naseby Hall, England, are among the many objects to be found on the first-floor galleries. On the second floor, several Russian icons of various designs from the fourteenth century through the eighteenth are depicted on several objects. An interesting patterned, marble bathtub of late first- or early second-century Rome is found here in addition to other early period objects. Many priceless objects are displayed on the third floor, such as the unique and beautifully carved sixteenth-century walnut door from Palermo, Sicily. Other treasures from Italy, Germany, Spain, and France are very well preserved for their great age.

At the top of the third-floor gallery is the Princess Zalessky Room containing a valuable exhibit, the major portion of which was a gift established by Princess Evangeline Zalstem-Zalessky. Among the objects of this exhibit is a seventeenth-century Brussels Renaissance tapestry in addition to other medieval objects and furniture. The windows of this room offer breathtaking views of the Atlantic Ocean and the breaking surf on the rocky shores far below.

On the way to the roof garden is the lower entrance hall, which displays a fine collection of old and rare silver spoons of various sizes, elaborately carved with detailed designs. The upper entrance hall to the outside roof garden contains some seventeenth-century furniture of interesting design in addition to Renaissance and Gothic chasubles.

Over a large, roof section of the southern portion of the castle is a skylight that covers a fifteenth-century French courtyard. The terrace room displays a Roman sarcophagus dating from the fifth to sixth centuries and carved of white marble. A set of eighty carved terra-cotta burial plaques, circa A.D. 300, are also shown in this room with other early period objects.

Hammond's vast collection of treasures within the castle museum is in itself a monumental effort. But this, too, includes the makeup of the castle with its various components of ancient architecture blended together in a pleasing order under one roof where one can easily find oneself walking into the past, to the Middle Ages and beyond.

Hammond was involved in the development of many national defense projects during World War II. In 1943 he developed the variable pitch propellor for ships and did pioneering work during both World Wars on radio dynamic torpedoes. Through the years he worked on many projects including single station broadcasting, in 1961, to any part of the globe and to outer space.

Hammond received many awards and belonged to various distinguished clubs and scientific societies, often serving as director or president. He was married to Irene Fenton, a young American artist and connoisseur of art. Mrs. Hammond was a most charming woman, tactful, a seasoned traveler, versed in astology, and skillful in gardening. Their long years of life together ended in 1959 when Mrs. Hammond passed away. Having no children, Mr. Hammond lived at the castle accompanied by a staff of servants. He usually worked at night, a habit he obtained from Alexander Graham Bell. He enjoyed the company of musicians, artists, actors, and playwrights, and had other personal interests including astrology, sailing, and world travel, and he also took part in some expeditions.

It was on February 12, 1965, that Hammond passed away, leaving his castle with its treasures as a dream fulfilled. The castle and its contents were bequeathed and exist today as the Hammond Museum, Incorporated, former home of famous inventor John

Hays Hammond, Jr., now owned by the Roman Catholic Archdiocese of Boston, Richard Cardinal Cushing, Trustee.

The castle is now open to visitors who may view the treasures of the museum and the various styles of ancient architecture that make up the castle struc-ture. The castle is open to group tours and daily tours conducted in the summer months. Frequent organ concerts are also given on the famous instrument whose sounds fill the Great Hall of Hammond Castle.

John Hays Hammond, Jr., outstanding inventor in electronics. Born April 13, 1888; died February 12, 1965. *Courtesy Hammond Museum, Inc.*

Towers of Hammond Castle, located in Gloucester, Massachusetts. Note the bay window at the upper left of the picture. *Courtesy Hammond Museum, Inc.*

The Great Hall is one hundred feet long and sixty feet high and occupies the central portion of the castle. To the right is seen the gilded woodcarving that surrounds the famous organ console. The bishop's stall is seen at the far end of the hall. *Courtesy Hammond Museum, Inc.*

The Great Hall chapel section was used by Hammond as a small reading or living room. *Courtesy Hammond Museum, Inc.*

This Gothic arched alcove off the Great Hall contains a treasure chest brought by the Moors to Spain but that is of Oriental origin. Inlaid stone and enamel pieces cover the exterior of the ancient chest. *Courtesy Hammond Museum, Inc.*

The refectory or dining room has a thirteenth-century tile floor and a fifteenth-century paneled ceiling made of 130 hand-painted wood pieces from Spain. *Courtesy Hammond Museum, Inc.*

Fifteenth-century black oak German Gothic credence. *Courtesy Hammond Museum, Inc.*

The marble bathtub is from Rome and is dated from the late first or early second century. The doorway is from eighth-century Italy. *Courtesy Hammond Museum, Inc.*

The Gothic Room with its bottle-glass window inserts contains many pieces of ancient furniture, such as the fourteenth-century Italian wrought-iron bed and the fifteenth-century Spanish dowry chest. *Courtesy Hammond Museum, Inc.*

The drawbridge leads to the front door of Hammond
Castle. *Courtesy Hammond Museum, Inc.*

House facade on the right side of the courtyard was once part of a merchant's house in Amiens about 1470. *Courtesy Hammond Museum, Inc.*

House facade from Tours. Upper portion of photo shows a thirteenth-century frieze of carved wood representing jugglers and acrobats. Facade is on left side of courtyard. *Courtesy Hammond Museum, Inc.*

] 2 [

PALMER CASTLE

BORN IN 1826, POTTER PALMER CAME TO CHIcago, Illinois, in 1852 from Albany County, New York, to seek his fortune in the dry goods business. But his life in Chicago was to leave a more permanent imprint on that city. Through his good common sense and splendid foresight his influence greatly aided in the destiny of the city's growth and development during its formative period. Palmer's efforts proved most successful with the opening of a store in the then fashionable retail mart on Lake Street.

Potter Palmer was a generation before his time in his new policies in merchandising, a situation that startled his competitors who predicted his ruin. At a time when the purchaser had to beware, Palmer inaugurated business ethics to an unheard of era of square dealing. A patron dealing at Palmer's store could actually exchange or have money refunded for goods purchased there. One could also take goods home for inspection before making an actual purchase.

The predicted ruin of Potter Palmer never took place. To the surprise of many, his business greatly prospered to the extent that after ten years he became known as the proprietor of the largest mercantile establishment in the Northwest.

Palmer later sold his interests to Field and Leiter, who conducted the establishment under that name. Upon completion of the transaction Palmer spent a season traveling through Europe, returning to Chicago where he invested heavily in real estate. Though

Lake Street was fashionable for shopping at that time, Palmer realized its limitations. A survey of the situation led him to purchase outright a mile of frontage along State Street, then a long, narrow road running north and south. As he rightly predicted the route was destined to be a much-traveled thoroughfare. He widened the road by twenty-seven feet and began erecting a row of buildings, including a hotel begun in 1869, named Palmer House. This eight-story building with its 225 rooms and salmon-colored walls was thought the last word in hotel achievement when it opened on September 26, 1871. Palmer often sent his personal note of welcome to special guests together with baskets of flowers and fruit.

In 1870, at the age of forty-four, Potter Palmer married Bertha Honore, a charming and very capable little woman one half his age who was born in Kentucky and raised in Illinois, and whose ancestry is traced to England and Charlemagne. Though things looked bright for the Palmers their hopes were soon to be shattered in the devastating Chicago Fire of October 8, 1871, only two weeks after the grand opening of Palmer House. The new hotel was reduced to ashes as was the entire mile of Palmer's buildings. It appeared then that his fortune had been lost forever. But his credit was sound, so sound that he was able to make a loan from a life insurance company for one million seven hundred thousand dollars, the largest individual loan ever recorded at that time. Two years later the hotel was rebuilt into a lavish edifice where it again prospered for its owner.

By 1882, Palmer was owner of several real estate holdings, among which were three thousand feet of frontage along a lake in a section of Chicago that was predicted would develop into the finest residential area in the city. A young and unknown firm of architects was engaged by Palmer to design a structure as a residence suitable to his position on the lakeshore site. The building was to comprise almost an entire city block with a frontage of 328 feet on Lake Shore Drive. It is curious that Palmer should consult with a relatively unknown architectural firm, but his choice proved to be an excellent one after all. The architects Henry Ives Cobb and Charles S. Frost evidently proposed a stone structure with an architectural style referred to as English battlemented and castellated Gothic in accordance to the desires of their client. This was to become the Palmer residence, a famous showplace and eventual landmark of the city for nearly seventy years.

In early March of 1882 a building permit notice was published, and in April the press was invited to see the plans of the building that was to cost nearly a quarter of a million dollars, an amount that increased to a million within a few years. No original drawings were preserved of the Palmer Castle, as it was to become known, with an attached mixture of praise and ridicule during its existence. By January, 1884, the basic construction was completed and contracts were issued to complete the interior rooms.

The basic structure, built of Connecticut brownstone and Amherst, Ohio, sandstone, was of three stories, eighty feet by fifty-six feet with exterior battlemented walls. A large and lofty square tower rose above the building, with an additional circular tower projecting from the northeast corner of the main tower and extending above it. Another smaller tower projected above the wall fronting a conservatory and was comparable in diameter to the circular tower facing the northeast corner of the building. The massiveness of the battlemented towers, rising majestically against the sky, was in contrast with the several ornate, petite turrets rising from the corners of the various wall facades.

Paired columns flanked the broad, impressive northeast entrance, whose location gave the structure a solid unity of the wall facades joining it from two opposite sides. The spacious loggia on the second floor facing the lake front also had solid columns between the first and third floors.

In contrast to the dark stone of the building, a lighter limestone trim created an extraordinary effect in pattern about the windows, towers, turrets, and battlements. This ornate trim was perhaps most effective in the spiral ribbon pattern around the circular northeast turret, bringing it to relief and contrasting it against the main square tower. This spiral trim together with the window locations of the turret gave evidence of the stairway within. The battlements crowning the walls, circular turrets, and towers, together with the columned entrance and solid facades, gave this massive castle structure a ruggedness of picturesque dignity found in the noble castles of European countries.

Through the diagonally located vestibule a central main hall was located, a feature permitting easy access to various rooms and a staircase to the upper floors. In addition to the vestibule and main hall, other rooms included the reception room, library, music room, drawing room, dining room, conservatory, art galleries, sitting rooms, bedrooms, and several other minor rooms such as a butler's pantry and storerooms.

Among the numerous features found throughout Palmer Castle was an elevator located just off the vestibule and believed to be the first elevator installed in a private residence in Chicago. The spacious rooms were elaborately finished and ornamented with much planning and exquisite craftsmanship. Friends of the Palmers were given the opportunity to inspect the magnificent residence when it was opened to them in 1885. Some of the rooms were altered at various periods in addition to the inclusion of another art gallery. Several valuable arts objects, sculptures, and numerous paintings were displayed in various rooms throughout the castle.

The porte cochere, with its wall above, and the driveway were moved several feet from their original position in order to provide an independent walkway for people to the main entrance.

The vestibule doors leading to the porte cochere were of large dimensions and contructed of solid mahogany. The vestibule floor, of marble mosaic, was bordered by a six-foot-high Siena marble wainscot. The ceiling was of the barrel-vaulted design of select mahogany. The richly colored materials of bronze metal grills, stained glass, and lunettes above mahogany side doors leading both to the elevator and circular tower stairs were greatly effective in enhancing the combined feeling of beauty and warmth to visitors entering this gracious residence.

The octagonal central hall, thirty feet across, was most spectacular in detailed design and perhaps is best described as having a variety in styles of architecture. Six doors of various panel designs led from this hall and conveniently provided access to other surrounding rooms. The floor was mosaicked in marble, and carved oak-paneled walls were ceiling high, with galleries or balconies supported by brackets of molded and carved fascias. Foliated ironwork filled the arches of the arcades, with carved, paneled balustrades, oriole-latticed niches, and stained-glass dome providing an impressive sight worthy of a detailed inspection viewed from below or from the galleries.

Through one of three columned arches forming the arcade to the west, a staircase led up to the galleries and upper floors. Carved panels formed the balustrades topped with heavy, wood rails connected to square, carved end posts with posts at intermediate landings supporting carved, seated-lion sculpture. Slender columns supported the grille-paneled arches of the galleries whose carvings and ironwork showed much detail. Other notable features were the four partly projecting, turned, latticed screens of Egyptian design that were built into and were part of the corners of the gallery walls. As carriages arrived bringing distinguished guests for an evening's entertainment at the castle, the Palmer children watched with fascination, peeping through the high fretwork at the corners of the second-floor gallery. It was not unusual to hear that the Palmers were giving a grand ball with a king or other royalty among the noted guests.

The reception room to the north was a somber chamber of teakwood providing a subdued background in contrast to the main hall. The general richness of the room in its hangings and carved panels created an atmosphere of restfulness for guests awaiting the greetings of the master.

A large drawing room or parlor adjoining the reception room also formed the northeast corner of the building. Facing north was a deep bay window, almost twenty feet long, of East Indian design, as were the carved teakwood walls and ceiling. This forty-two- by twenty-two-foot room was richly adorned with bronze and silver chandeliers and stamped leather panels, with rich fabrics creating and completing the Oriental setting of the room.

By 1887 plans for redesign of the Indian drawing room were underway because the present design was thought by the owners to be too somber. The redesign called for a Louis XIV style with additions in ornamentation and delicate mosaic patterns in the fireplace. The ceiling was of an elaborate design with murals representing cherubs pictured in various activities amidst a cloud-furled design.

The library, facing the lake, was a most impressive room of Flemish Renaissance with an abundance of fine, detailed carvings throughout. The carved fireplace mantle supported six oak, sculptured, female figures, each five feet in height, four of which fronted the chimney piece and two on the sides. The walls on either side of the fireplace contained windows whose upper portions enclosed beautifully designed, perforated panels. Carved panels separated the bookcases that lined the walls to a height of easy access, with a frieze bordering their tops, forming an insert shelf supporting small carved columns spaced at varying intervals. The wide upper portions of the curved walls that met the ceiling were intricately carved, and frame-painted murals of various lengths represented scenes of literary characters. The English oak ceiling contained carved inset panels, and spanning the ceiling separating the bay windows was a carved beam whose ends rested on slender columns of carved, spiral design.

Of Moorish design, the morning or music room to the south was finished in flat cherry, which created and enhanced the effective coloring of the rooms under soft lighting. The southwest corner was occupied by windows that opened into the conservatory with its marble walks and luxuriant tropical plants. Access to the conservatory was from the dining room, which also adjoined the morning room.

The dining room to the southwest of the main hall was a spacious room measuring twenty-four by thirty-two feet and was finished in polished mahogany. Rising above the parquetry floor were the sideboards of a nine-foot wainscot found on four sides of this octagonal room. Intricately carved ceiling panels joined the darker wood of the carved cornice that bordered the upper walls. Between the cornice and the wainscot was a wide space occupied by an oil-painted mural frieze by the American artist John Elliott. These paintings gracefully illustrated varied actions of cupids amidst an autumnal pastoral setting on a golden background. The west wall was occupied by a chimney piece with a carved mantel shelf and arched, mirrored panels. The richness of this room with its fluted columns, Elizabethan sideboards, and free-standing arches with foliated spandrels, was indeed a magnificent representation of interior decoration. Beyond the dining room to the west were service rooms for stores, a butler's pantry, and the back stairway.

The elevator off the vestibule provided easy access to Mrs. Palmer's bedroom apartment on the second floor. This luxurious chamber, of Moorish design, had oil-painted walls above a four-foot-high paneled wainscot and a beautifully carved, wood-paneled ceiling. Ebony and gold were used in the woodwork, and colored glass filled the upper arches of latticed windows. With its gold and garnet glass chandeliers, ornamented tiles of the wainscoted dressing room, and sunken tub of the bath, this Oriental chamber indeed offered a service and repose to its occupant.

Built across the west or rear side of the building and maintaining its original design, an art gallery was constructed with a separate north entrance. The gallery also provided an additional service for holding banquets and balls, and was divided into three parts called the Main Gallery, East Gallery, and South Gallery. The large Main Gallery measured seventy-one by thirty-seven feet with a high ceiling enabling the additional facility of a musicians' balcony located above the east entrance. Above the red-marble wainscot, velvet-covered walls reached to the bordered cornice and served as a background for displaying paintings in heavy, gold frames. An interesting feature of the gallery was the large canopy screen with hanging electric lights about its perimeter to constantly direct light on the numerous paintings. Smooth-surfaced, Greek ionic marble columns were located at the east and south walls, two of which flanked the entrance to the adjoining gallery.

The South Gallery measured forty by twenty-two feet and the East Gallery, with its gold mosaic wainscot, measured thirty-two by sixteen feet. Both of these smaller galleries had marble mosaic floors and were at a slightly higher elevation that the Main Gallery, but at an even level with adjoining rooms. It was in these galleries that the paintings of Corot,

Monet, Millet, Innes, Pissaro, and other masters were exhibited.

Over the years Palmer Castle had other additions and alterations by successive architects and decorators. The treatment of its various other chambers throughout this massive structure was also not lacking in architectural refinement. Palmer's Castle soon became the showplace of the city and was one of the first famous residences to be erected in what was then becoming Chicago's new, exclusive residential section.

To support and in keeping with the grandeur of the castle, its social history was no less brilliant, especially during the time of the World's Columbian Exposition of 1893, of which Mrs. Palmer was president of the board of lady managers. Among the guests of the castle were presidents of the United States Grant, Garfield, and McKinley, and the Prince of Wales, who later became King Edward VII. The Infanta Eulalia of Spain was also a guest, as were various Russian princes and princesses, and many other persons of nobility and leading figures of Victorian society.

It was in this period of Middle West history that Bertha Palmer ruled in undisputed social supremacy throughout the balance of her lifetime. Palmer Castle was the hub of social life, especially at the New Year's Eve balls. To receive an invitation to such a notable event meant you were considered "in" Chicago society for the following year because Mrs. Palmer had put her stamp of approval on you. She granted audience by appointments in writing, even to her closest friends. Such appointments were passed through twenty-seven hands that included butlers, maids, and social secretaries in that order.

Mrs. Palmer usually presided alone at stately dinners because her husband, absorbed in his numerous business affairs, was reluctant to be called a "society man." Often gowned in regal black velvet, wearing her famous thirty-thousand-dollar diamond tiara and a rope of pearls, Bertha Palmer did not merely enter a room, she made an entrance. Her remoteness, carefully controlled voice, beauty, brilliant mind, and dazzling personality awed all with whom she came in contact.

On May 4, 1902, Potter Palmer died, leaving his children and Mrs. Palmer, who continued to live in the castle and who managed her late husband's business enterprises. She also became a noted collector of art, with European and American masterpieces adorning the velvet walls of the castle's art galleries. Mrs. Palmer also maintained residences in Paris and London, and was as well known in European circles of society as she was in America. In 1918, this gracious lady, who was once a dominant figure of brilliant society, passed away. The castle was abandoned until 1921, when Potter Palmer, Jr. remodeled and redecorated the interior of the castle and took up residence there with his family.

In 1928 the castle was sold to Vincent Bendix, head of the Bendix Aviation Corporation. He used the castle as a residence and private art gallery. During this period the castle was opened briefly to the public for a two-day charity benefit, with crowds of curious people coming to gaze at the awesome splendor of the castle's interior and wondrous architectural beauty, a tribute to craftsmanship and design. In 1933, after the depression had struck, Bendix conveyed the property back to Palmer, Jr. The last great party held at the castle was given in 1935 for Pauline, the daughter of Palmer, Jr. The castle was again unoccupied for a time but was used by the Red Cross during World War II as a major surgical dressing center.

But like other similar structures whose architectural significance labeled them as familiar landmarks to thousands of people, this magnificent building, among the most brilliant in American architectural history, was destined to the fate of the bulldozer. In 1945 the castle was sold to a New York syndicate that had plans for erecting large apartment buildings on the site. The castle was held under lease by the Palmers until 1950, and in mid-1949 a sale of furnishings remaining in the residence was held on the premises.

In early February of 1951 official razing of the Palmer Castle was begun, thus ending an era of the grand style and manner of life that once existed in American society in so many forgotten places.

Palmer Castle, about 1890. Formerly located in Chicago, Illinois, on Lake Shore Drive, the castle's social history was at its peak during the 1893 World's Columbian Exposition. Presidents, nobility, and other leading figures of Victorian society were guests. The castle's main entrance and tower are clearly viewed in this picture. *Courtesy Chicago Historical Society.*

Palmer Castle, about 1905. The people in the horse-driven buggy may be viewing either the castle or the new automobile that is parked under the porte cochere. The large conservatory on the south side of the castle housed luxuriant tropical plants. *Courtesy Chicago Historical Society.*

The octagonal main central hall provided easy access to the surrounding rooms. The staircase at the far end of the photo shows carved panels viewed through the center arcade. *Courtesy Chicago Historical Society.*

The stairwell at one end of the main central hall shows carved paneling of the balustrade. Note the grillwork of the arcades and the design of the slender columns. *Courtesy Chicago Historical Society.*

The central hall, showing intricate carvings on the woodwork. Dragon-ornamented chandeliers hang from brackets on panels below the Egyptian latticed screens. The library is seen through the open doorway. *Courtesy Chicago Historical Society.*

The second-floor stairwell shows elaborate carvings on all portions of this gallery and the staircase leading to the upper floors. *Courtesy Chicago Historical Society.*

The library, showing the fireplace with its oak, sculptured figures, and carved mantle. *Courtesy Chicago Historical Society.*

View of the northeast corner of the library. Large, elaborate chandeliers hang from the carved, paneled ceiling. *Courtesy Chicago Historical Society.*

This portion of the library shows the carved upper portions of the wall with one of the painted murals. The perforated carved panels decorate the upper window casements. *Courtesy Chicago Historical Society.*

Drawing room, east end, altered from eighteenth-century French to eighteenth-century English in 1921. *Courtesy Chicago Historical Society.*

Drawing room showing wall screens. Altered in 1921. *Courtesy Chicago Historical Society.*

One of the many bedrooms of Palmer Castle. *Courtesy Chicago Historical Society.*

The main gallery of Palmer Castle. The absence of the canopy shows the large skylight and suspended electric lights. Many valuable paintings hung from the velvet-covered walls that served as a background for the gold-framed masterpieces. *Courtesy Chicago Historical Society.*

] 3 [

LAMBERT CASTLE

LAMBERT CASTLE, LOCATED AT PATERSON, NEW Jersey, was planned and built by Catholina Lambert in 1892. Lambert was born at Keighley, in Yorkshire, England, on March 28, 1834, and at the early age of ten he started working in a cotton mill where his seventy-two hours of weekly labor paid him thirty-two cents in equivalent American money. It was during these early years as a poor delivery boy that he was often sent to Warwick Castle to deliver goods, and he dreamed of building such a castle in the hopeful success of his life.

At the age of seventeen he journeyed to New York City, arriving there in late October of 1851. Having a friend in Boston, Massachusetts, he immediately went to that city, where he found employment as an office boy in the silk firm of Tilt and Dexter. He saved what he could of his earnings, and in 1853, when Tilt retired from the small firm, young Lambert bought the retired gentleman's share in the firm, which became Dexter, Lambert and Company, until its termination over sixty years later. The firm is credited as having been the first to weave ribbon in America, though earlier experiments in 1849 and 1856 were not successful. The firm's first factory, located in Boston, was a two-story frame building with weaving machines that produced upholstery, fringes, millinery, parasols, cloak and dress trimmings, braiding, and several other such items. In 1856, a second, larger mill factory was erected in Boston, but by 1860 the silk

manufacturing center was in Paterson, New Jersey, which brought Lambert to that city on frequent business trips. While there, Lambert saw and greatly admired the natural beauty in the region of Passaic Valley and Garret Mountain. In 1861 he purchased a twenty-two-acre farm called Maplewood in South Paterson, where he, his wife Isabella, and their daughter took up residence.

At that same time Anson Dexter retired from the firm but was replaced by his son, who later retired in 1875. Lambert's younger brother, William, also entered the growing silk firm, but he died in South America in 1869 during a visit there. During the following years the firm purchased and built other plants in various places in addition to having other partners associated with it. Once of the last large mills, located at Homesdale, Pennsylvania, was erected in 1887 with the firm now manufacturing silk of wide varieties from raw material.

In addition to Lambert's business interests, he was a great collector of art, with his chief interest in fine paintings and statuary items. He also planned to build a castellated residence, perhaps partly to house his growing art collection and also to fulfill his boyhood dreams, as the structure was said to resemble Warwick Castle in England to some degree. Construction of the new residence began in 1892 with local quarries being used to obtain the brownstone that stonecutters assembled in large blocks. Work on the castle must have proceeded with great vigor, because the structure was completed by the end of that same year. In 1893 Lambert and his family established their residence at the castle, which he named Belle Vista, after his wife Isabella.

The stately architecture of Belle Vista was further enhanced shortly after its completion with the addition of a magnificent art gallery, which extended on the original north end of the castle. Nearing the completion of the new art gallery in midyear of 1896, Lambert had a seventy-foot-high castle tower built on the summit of Garret Mountain, which was used as an observatory and summer house. The tower was made accessible by a winding carriage driveway that was constructed up the mountain, whose elevation gave a magnificent view of the surrounding valleys and hills of the countryside.

Lambert Castle is primarily on three stories with a basement floor, and several battlemented towers and turrets. A white, stone trim lines the various floor level and towers, with battlements also in this contrasting white stone. A long retaining wall of stone similar to the castle appears to elevate the entire castle above the lower grounds to the right of the main entrance. Some arched windows are found on the upper story of the projected rooms to the right of the main entrance, but the majority of the windows are uniformly rectangular with smaller windows found at various locations throughout the castle.

The principal rooms in Lambert Castle, in addition to the new art gallery, included an entrance hall, reception room, drawing room, dining room, main art gallery, art gallery hall, ballroom, music room, breakfast room, family rooms, and guest quarters. A grand staircase gave access to the art gallery on the second floor, which was also occupied by the family's living quarters, the Gem Room, and a spacious guest chamber. Servants' quarters on the castle's west side were separately connected to the building.

The entrance hall displayed columns of sixteenth-century Italian carvings finished in gold and black. Fine quality oak, expertly finished, was used in the woodwork of all rooms throughout the castle.

Located next to the music room, on the first floor of the tower, was the circular drawing room, similar in design to that in Windsor Castle. An oil painting by the Austrian decorator L. Leistner is displayed on the ceiling with a glass chandelier of Bohemian origin, still intact. An elaborately carved, Italian tulipwood mantlepiece, finished in gold and black, remains in this room, which was furnished in the style of Louis XV, with some additional rare furniture and Chinese vases.

The dining room ceiling has delicate, carved designs in panels varying in dimensions. From the large center panel once hung a beautifully designed, French bronze chandelier. A square-patterned, oak-paneled wainscot occupies the lower half of the walls, whose upper portions displayed fine paintings in heavy gold frames. The exquisite hand-carved work of the sixteenth-century Italian furniture in this room was said to be the finest in America.

Located in the northwest wing of the castle was the beautiful breakfast room with walls displaying paintings by such artists as Renoir and Monet. One wall was entirely covered by a large, plate-glass mirror enclosed in a bower supported by two pairs of highly ornate columns. Two of these columns came from Pisa and are of Italian Renaissance design, while the other two are spiral copies depicting similar columns in front of Rome's St. Peter's Cathedral. Fronting this great mirror was an interesting latticed grillwork giving a floral effect with vines and roses. The overall effect of this wall was one of delicate beauty ornamented with pieces of fine art objects. With furniture entirely in turquoise and gold, the features of this room presented it as one of the most interesting in the castle.

The music room, with its marble floor, once echoed with the sounds of a fine string orchestra seated behind potted, exotic plants and ferns. Fine paintings of such artists as Montecelli adorned the walls and hung over the mantelpiece. Lambert's library, also used as his office, contained numerous heavy, gold-framed paintings surrounding the carved furniture, glass-fronted bookcases, interesting chandelier, and oak mantel over an ornate fireplace grille.

The castle's main hall continued through the grand art hall with its flooring laid in square, marble blocks that once were covered with fine rugs. The grand art gallery was a high room extending three stories to the ceiling dome. Balconied galleries on the second and third floors, with fronts festooned in carved, floral designs, overlooked the main gallery room. The upper gallery level was also once occupied by musicians who played at receptions at the castle.

The first housewarming reception held at Lambert

Castle was on the last day of January, 1893. The reception was a magnificent event with the castle prepared in floral decorations and myriads of brilliantly illuminated electric lights placed throughout the castle and its exterior towers making it visible for miles around. A special railroad train from Jersey City and hundreds of carriages brought many of the four hundred invited guests to and from the castle. The arrival of the carriages winding up the driveway to the brilliantly lit castle was a most picturesque and romantic scene. The guests were received by the Lamberts in the reception room with the entire castle thrown open for visitation. At the time of this reception Lambert had an immense art collection of considerable value rated as the finest in the country and above any individual collection in his native England. The new art gallery addition, completed in 1896, displayed a large variety of fine paintings and statuary in its one hundred by thirty-five feet of space. Skylights and special electric lights were carefully placed along the gallery with its graceful wood, open-arched framing spaced at wide intervals.

To celebrate the opening of the new art gallery, Lambert, who was a gracious host, held a grand art reception on February 25, 1896, providing special trains for the eight hundred invited guests. Two bands of musicians, one a Hungarian Gypsy band from New York stationed in the music room, the other, Haase's State Band posted in the upper gallery level of the main art gallery room, provided concert music for the guests, who included many prominent persons of that time. Among the many visitors to Lambert Castle were President McKinley and Vice-President Hobart, both viewing with admiration the stately castle and its magnificent art collection during their visit on September 5, 1898. There were numerous visitors whom Lambert personally escorted throughout the castle. He took great pride especially in showing the art galleries and was always an equally kind host regardless of the varying prominence of his guests.

In 1901 Lambert was widowed with the death of his wife, Isabella. He later married Harriet Estelle, sister of Isabella and herself a widow with a son, Major Harry Bibby, who managed for several years the affairs of Dexter, Lambert and Company of Pennsylvania. It is interesting to note that Lambert's name was used for various local telephone exchanges in Paterson.

The labor troubles of 1913 had their effect in Paterson as they did elsewhere. By 1914 the strain on the silk business caused great financial difficulties for Lambert's firm as it had on other companies. In late October, 1914, Lambert was able to obtain an extension of credit, signing two-year notes with his entire estate as collateral. Since the estate included Lambert's valuable art collection, it was later decided to auction some 365 paintings and several pieces of the fine statuary. The grand auction, held in New York City for four days in late February of 1916, resulted in over half a million dollars, a price said to be only one-third the real value of the auctioned art treasures.

Lambert had felt the pangs of sorrow at various periods of the previous ten years, and more with the death of seven of his eight children. On November 27, 1916, he was further sorrowed with the death of his wife Harriet. Of his once large family, only he and his son, Walter S. Lambert, remained.

As the years passed, Lambert continued to busy himself in the silk manufacturing business and his favorite interests in art. At two o'clock on the afternoon of February 15, 1923, the nearly eighty-nine-year-old Lambert took to his bed after having spent the earlier part of the day in the castle's library discussing the silk business with his brother-in-law. Within two hours after he went to his bedchamber, Catholina Lambert peacefully passed away with his son, Walter, and personal physician at his bedside. Funeral services were held on the eighteenth of February with interment made in the family plot. The services were attended by hundreds of prominent persons, among whom was the United States attorney general.

Walter Lambert had also lived at the castle with his wife and family. After the death of his father he placed the estate for sale, thus ending family life at the castle. In 1925, the city of Paterson purchased the castle at public sale using it as a health institution for the Paterson Tuberculosis Health League. A few years later the Passaic County Park System was established with various projects that included the acquisition of the Garret Mountain Reservation. By November, 1928, some 575 acres of property, including Lambert Castle, were acquired.

The fall of 1934 marked the end of extensive renovations to Lambert Castle, which included the removal of the whole north end of the structure, leaving the castle as it originally appeared in 1893. Just prior to the alterations, the Passaic County Historical Society was invited to use the castle's first floor in establishing its local historical museum there. This was done at the instance of the then president of the Passaic County Park Commission, Garret A. Hobart. Other floors of the castle were reserved for business and caretaker's use.

With the establishment of the museum at Lambert Castle and the generous aid of Mrs. Hobart, Sr., the Passaic County Historical Society had on display a most complete collection of documents and numerous other items covering America's history from 1896 to 1901, in the McKinley-Hobart Room. Lambert's old drawing room, now occupied by the McKinley-Hobart Room, displays a variety of handsome antique furniture and other notable items in its display cases.

The magnificent music room has several display cases covering three hundred years of Passaic Valley culture in its fine collection. As with the chandelier in the entrance hall, the chandeliers in the music room and the McKinley-Hobart Room are the only remaining original fixtures.

Lambert's former library and office room is used as the museum's library, also called the Founder's Room. Its numerous bookcases are filled with hundreds of fine volumes, including Passaic County directories that start from 1824. Many years ago Lambert gave permission to a movie company to use the castle as a location for a motion picture. One day when entering this room Lambert was astounded to find a lady napping on his couch. He had not expected such a domestic invasion, but with apologies and introductions made by the movie manager he finally learned that the girl was Pearl White, the famous movie actress then filming one of the thrilling series of the *Perils of Pauline*.

The outer entrance hall and ballroom contain several fine paintings, one of the Passaic Falls chasm that is believed to date about 1810. The magnificent dining room remains as Lambert knew it, with the exception of the furniture and the chandelier, which were removed. It is now the main display case room, where numerous objects of local history and antique furniture are exhibited, including an Edison phonograph exhibit of 1878 to 1912.

Lambert Castle remains in excellent condition as the museum headquarters of the Passaic County Historical Society. The battlements, turrets, and towers of this noble structure still give evidence of the dream of a poor young boy who long ago envisioned his Warwick Castle in America and made it come true.

Catholina Lambert in later years. *Courtesy The Passaic County Historical Society*.

East view of Lambert Castle as it appeared in 1893.
Courtesy The Passaic County Historical Society.

Main entrance of Lambert Castle as it appeared in
1893. This portion of the castle remains the same today.
Courtesy The Passaic County Historical Society.

Lambert Castle in 1896. This east view shows the addition to the right of the three story circular tower. This added section was removed in later years. *Courtesy The Passaic County Historical Society.*

The drawing room in 1893, looking toward the main art gallery. This is now the McKinley-Hobart Room. *Courtesy The Passaic County Historical Society.*

The castle's dining room as it appeared in 1893. The furniture is long since gone, but the room with its carved, paneled ceiling remains. *Courtesy The Passaic County Historical Society.*

1893 view of the breakfast room showing latticed grillwork. This room was furnished entirely in turquoise and gold. *Courtesy The Passaic County Historical Society.*

The main art gallery as it appeared in 1893. This west wall and side view show a portion of the upper galleries. *Courtesy The Passaic County Historical Society.*

Lambert's library and office in 1893. *Courtesy The Passaic County Historical Society*.

The new art gallery as it appeared in 1896. The Pandora statue (first on right) was returned to the castle in 1948 as a gift. It now stands in the castle hall. *Courtesy The Passaic County Historical Society*.

View of the castle's north garden in 1896. *Courtesy The Passaic County Historical Society.*

The McKinley-Hobart Room with display cases as viewed today. *Courtesy The Passaic County Historical Society.*

The music room with museum display cases as seen today. *Courtesy The Passaic County Historical Society.*

] 4 [
GELSTON CASTLE

OVERLOOKING THE MOHAWK VALLEY NEAR MO-hawk, New York, stands a fine old structure called Gelston Castle. This castle, also previously known as Cruger Mansion and Henderson House, was built in 1832 by Harriet Douglas Cruger, as a faithful repro-duction of her ancestral home, Gelston Castle, in Scotland.

The original property consisted of a land grant of sixteen thousand acres made to Dr. James Hender-son in 1739 by George II of England. The vast acre-age of natural wilderness was not used until Mrs. George Douglas, granddaughter of Dr. Henderson, erected the original homestead on the property in 1787. This enlarged, seventeen-room framed home still remains on the present 350-acre property where the castle is also situated. Mrs. Douglas's daughter, Harriet, a sister-in-law of President James Monroe, was presented to the court of William IV, and dur-ing that time visited Gelston Castle, which belonged to her uncle. Harriet, then a very wealthy young heiress, was so delighted with her uncle's Scottish castle that she decided to duplicate the castle as a home on her American country estate in Herkimer County, New York. The present 350-acre property site consisted mainly of farmland and pastures, in-cluding about 150 acres of woodlands and a small forty-foot-deep lake approximately two hundred by five hundred feet in dimension used for swimming, boating, and fishing.

Cut grey stone for the castle's thirty-inch-thick walls was obtained from Little Falls quarries and hauled over snow lands by sledge fourteen miles to the hilltop site of construction. The finished castle, complete with battlements and turrets, contains twenty-two spacious rooms, some of which make up the rounded wings of the castle that is surrounded by a dry moat enclosure behind an ornamented wrought-iron fence. Some of the castle's more prominent rooms are the great hall, drawing room, and library. Other rooms include ten master bedrooms, seven servants bedrooms, and a large variety of service rooms. Elaborate crystal chandeliers were imported from abroad and shipped up the Hudson River to Albany, then transported overland through eighty miles of forest to the castle. The castle was kept in excellent condition throughout those years with a pleasing growth of ivy gradually covering some of its old walls.

But the peace and tranquillity of the place as pic-tured from without its old walls did not always exist within. One of the stories about the castle tells of Harriet, who was estranged from her husband. Upon returning from England she found her husband liv-ing at the castle fighting for his marital rights. En-raged at the predicament, she took up residence in the original homestead next to the castle she loved so much. Being somewhat of a celebrity chaser, she was much annoyed at having James Fenimore Cooper deliberately avoid her, riding past her home to visit with her husband, writing and enjoying the comforts of the castle.

The two-story central portion of the castle, with its main entrance, has a low-pitched roof with two adjoining wings on either side, each two stories high, with attractive curved end bays. Additional lower wings, with projected front facades and rounded side bays, adjoin the two-story inner wings, giving balance to the entire imposing structure. The windows are generally rectangular with upper story windows being shorter in height than those of the lower floors. Full-length louvered shutters open out on all first-floor windows. Several crenellated chimney pieces rise above the roof levels, protruding slightly from the exterior walls as they rise in a uniform manner. The flat roofs of the high inner wings and outer lower wing extensions have uniformly designed perimeter railings enclosing spacious deck areas that give excellent views of the surrounding countryside. Spacious broad decks are located at various places around the castle, with stairways leading down to the lawns and gardens that cover some five acres.

The numerous chimneys give evidence of the castle's twenty-one fireplaces located in almost every room. These fireplaces vary in design and materials, being of marble, wood, and some brick. One of the brick fireplaces, uncovered in the basement kitchen wall, was an original cooking fireplace to the castle. Marble mantels were imported from Scotland at the time the castle was built.

The first floor contains the great hall, a large fifty-by-twenty-foot room with a ten-foot-high arched ceiling. This room is also used as a dining room and features a beautiful marble fireplace detailed with carved American eagles on columns flanking a small, carved, central design of human figures. This unique fireplace, with the present owner's beautiful antiques on its mantel, is located in the semicircular alcove with high French windows on each side. Also found in this room is a rare, Robson pipe organ built before 1820 and brought over from England many years ago. Suspended from the ceiling by four chains is the present owner's addition of a unique ship chandelier detailed with individual glass pieces that make up the ship's hull and stern cabin windows. When lighted by the enclosed electric lamp the effect of its light is gay and tranquil.

The twenty-eight-by-twenty drawing room also contains a beautiful, highly carved, marble fireplace located in a similar manner as the one in the great hall. Over the mantel is a beautifully carved, gold-framed, French mirror, purchased when the castle was originally furnished. The exquisite, ornate chandelier in this part of the room is also from that early period. Never having been electrified, it remains in its original beautiful condition. French windows flank the fireplace with five such windows opening to spacious porches. A recent addition of stained-glass panels hang from upper recesses of the French windows. Both the great hall and drawing room have oak floors with parquet borders giving added beauty to these interesting rooms.

The library measures sixteen feet square and also contains a carved mantel fireplace. Bookcases on the walls are matched with adjoining display shelves fronted with long, glass doors. Other rooms on this floor are two master bedrooms, each twenty-two by sixteen feet, both with fireplaces and baths, a study or office, a maid's room with a bath, and service rooms. One of the dining rooms displays a collection of heavy copperware in addition to early pieces of dining furniture.

The second floor contains four master bedrooms, the largest measuring twenty-five by seventeen feet, all with fireplaces and baths. An additional four smaller, paired bedrooms are also located on this floor, each pair being of equal dimension, with the largest pair measuring twenty-five by ten feet.

A large basement contains a twenty-by-sixteen foot kitchen with dumbwaiter service facilities. The original brick cooking fireplace has a wood mantel displaying the present owner's fine collection of antique mugs. Six bedrooms, a bath, and a twenty-five-by-sixteen-foot sitting room were for the help that once occupied these quarters. A laundry room, in addition to furnace rooms with an oil-steam heating unit and a coal furnace, also occupies a part of the basement.

Other numerous and well-equipped structures are found on the property in addition to the castle and the original homestead structure. Such buildings include an oil-heated, nine-room gate house, several large garage buildings, three large barns, an eighteen-by-twelve-foot boathouse with dock, water tower, 250-foot-deep water well, and greenhouse measuring fifty by sixteen feet with a twenty-by-ten-foot potting shed. One of the barns contains several carriages, including the one used by Theodore Roosevelt, who drove alone about the grounds when visiting his sister, the wife of Douglas Robinson, Under-secretary of the Navy.

When Harriet Cruger died, she willed the property to Fanny Monroe, and until 1966 the castle remained with various members of the family, the most recent being the Douglas and Robinson families whose descendants were first granted the original property in 1739. The castle has also been a home and frequented recreational place to many distinguished persons related to its former owners, such as President Theodore Roosevelt and President Franklin D. Roosevelt. It is said that many New York State and national political deals were shaped behind the closed doors of the castle.

Gelston Castle had been unoccupied since July, 1962, until it was sold for the first time to a person outside the family. In 1966 Mrs. Jan Blair purchased the castle estate with plans that it be restored to its original significance and as a home with facilities for varied recreational activities attractively suited to elderly and handicapped women. The original owners have retained their fenced seventy-five-square-foot family cemetery plot with access to it for members of the family. Below the tennis court is a pet cemetery with several little marble headstones for animals belonging to previous occupants.

When Mrs. Blair obtained the property it had been grossly neglected. "Everything was horrible to touch or look at. Mildew had turned white walls absolutely black. Vandals had smashed glass, painted things on the walls and floors, but fortunately had not damaged the lovely fireplaces or the chandeliers." The renovations to restore the castle were considerable with repairs made to the cracked walls and a new roof added. Fortunately, the floor construction was still in excellent condition, but new plumbing and rewiring was required and completed. Many months passed before curved plate glass could be specially made, at considerable expense, to replace the castle's broken windowpanes.

The original furniture was gone, with the exception of the pipe organ, which still plays, and the delicate chandeliers, French mirror, and handmade drapery poles in the drawing room. The fine furniture pieces now at the castle are mostly beautiful antiques of Mrs. Blair and her family. A few modern additions to the castle include freezing and refrigeration units, a private dining room, and basement kilns for the ceramic occupational therapy crafts produced by the elderly women at the castle.

Mrs. Blair's tremendous program of occupational therapy does not give evidence of the castle as being a retirement home or a nursing home. The care given to the castle's elderly occupants is one that makes them feel they are needed and are leading useful lives. In addition to classes in ceramics, other activities include stained-glass painting, dressmaking, woodworking, embroidery, and other active projects. The women have joined local organizations for socialization and craft work. Tennis and horseback riding are among the sports activities and, if they desire, the women are allowed to cook and bake specialties with delicious results the whole household delights and enjoys. Pageant costumes are made for special occasions, and church services are held in the castle's drawing room by a local pastor.

The restorations made to the castle by Mrs. Blair have greatly enhanced this lovely place with its former significance and quiet, stately beauty.

From its high vantage point, Gelston Castle commands a panoramic view of the peaks of the distant Adirondacks across the broad Mohawk Valley. The castle now retains the Old-World charm and architectural beauty that it had when young Harriet Douglas Cruger first conceived the transformation of her Scottish ancestral home on American soil in 1832.

Gelston Castle was constructed in 1832 at Mohawk, New York. The main entry is at the left of the photo. Note the round end bays and crenellated chimney shafts. *Courtesy Previews, Incorporated, New York.*

Front view of Gelston Castle showing the round end bays flanking the centrally located entrance. *Courtesy Mrs. Jan Blair.*

The Robson pipe organ in the great hall is a rare
instrument built in England before 1820. The room
pictured here is as it exists today. *Alan Studio, Inc.,
courtesy Mrs. Jan Blair.*

The ship chandelier in the great hall is a unique fixture with individual glass pieces making up the hull and stern cabin windows. Electrically lighted, its glow is gay and tranquil. *Alan Studio, Inc., courtesy Mrs. Jan Blair.*

This magnificent carved marble fireplace is located in one of the round end bay windows of the great hall. The antiques are those of the present owner of the castle. *Alan Studio, Inc., courtesy Mrs. Jan Blair.*

Portion of the drawing room at the curved end bay shows a highly carved fireplace with the original French mirror above the mantle. The drapery poles and ornate chandelier are also originally from an early period. The stained-glass panels were installed by the present owner. *Alan Studio, Inc., courtesy Mrs. Jan Blair.*

An original cooking fireplace of the castle uncovered by the present owner. *Alan Studio, Inc., courtesy Mrs. Jan Blair.*

This dining room displays a copper collection and early furniture. *Alan Studio, Inc., courtesy Mrs. Jan Blair.*

This marble fireplace of the library has a mantel display of antiques. *Alan Studio, Inc., courtesy Mrs. Jan Blair.*

] 5 [
VIKINGSHOLM CASTLE

IT WAS IN 1928 THAT MRS. LORA JOSEPHINE Knight, a gracious lady of New England ancestry, purchased about two hundred acres of an isolated land site at Emerald Bay in the lovely Lake Tahoe region of California. This grand place of massive evergreen trees and mountain scenery of Northern California and the Sierras, was to be the location of a unique architectural structure in this country that would blend into the magnificent scenery.

Born Lora Josephine Small, on May 1, 1864, in Galena, Illinois, her long line of distinguished descendents in America trace back to those who came with the Mayflower. Lora Josephine attended the public schools in Galena until the family moved to Chicago, where she continued her education in a private school. After the death of her father in 1882, Lora's mother took her children to their summer home in the town of Geneva on the Fox River.

On April 26, 1883, Lora Josephine married James Hobart Moore, a well-known lawyer who formed a partnership with his brother, gaining distinguished international reputation as organizers of vast business interests under the name of "The Moore Brothers." Lora and her husband lived in Chicago for some time after their marriage, later taking up residence on the shore of Lake Geneva, Wisconsin, where Moore built a home on a large tract of land he had purchased there. They spent many happy years at Lake Geneva, where they established stables for thoroughbred horses, won numer-

ous prizes at horticulture shows, and entertained their guests in their small steam yacht on the lake.

Due to failing health and the severe winter climate, Mr. and Mrs. Moore purchased a winter home at Montecito, a section of Santa Barbara, in Southern California, where they spent most of their time each year. In early June, 1916 Moore became more seriously ill. He insisted on returning to their Lake Geneva home where, on July 17, 1916, he passed away.

Selling the Lake Geneva property, the widowed Mrs. Moore continued her residence in her home at Montecito. Being a generous, public-spirited person, she established a school for Mexican children, who were taught by skilled teachers.

On January 18, 1922, Mrs. Moore married Harry French Knight, of St. Louis, Missouri. Disposing of her Montecito property, she and her husband built a new home in Santa Barbara, where they spent the winter months. In 1926 Mrs. Knight and her sister, Mrs. William H. Moore, made an extensive worldwide tour in the private yacht *Alacrity,* visiting such places as India, Africa, South America, and numerous other ports seldom visited by the regular traveler. This tour was only one of many such tours that Mrs. Knight made during her lifetime.

At about the time Mrs. Knight acquired her Lake Tahoe property, the Swedish architect Lennart Palme married into her family. Palme was born in Stockholm, Sweden, on January 16, 1881. Graduating in

Stockholm as a civil engineer, Palme practiced as engineer and architect in Stockholm and Helsinfos, Finland, constructing several large office buildings, apartment houses, theaters, and numerous other structures. Palme's father was well known as the founder of *Stockhomes Intecknings Garanti, A.B.,* a large bank in Stockholm of which he was president for fifty years.

Mrs. Knight was influenced by a structure of Swedish design that Palme had built in New York, and in the summer of 1928 she invited Palme and his wife to accompany her on an extensive architectural exploration trip throughout Scandinavia. This journey was to gather ideas for a structure of Scandinavian influence that Mrs. Knight desired to build. During the trip Mrs. Knight selected furniture for her future home to be reproduced, since several of the displayed antiques she wanted could not be imported.

On returning home, Mrs. Knight decided on a commodious structure that would also incorporate the atmosphere and design of an old Viking castle of stone construction. She chose this style of architecture as being suitable and harmonious with the rugged landscape, high mountains, and big trees, rather than another more sophisticated style of architecture. The castle, built in the shape of a horseshoe with two wings enclosing a courtyard, was to be placed among the trees without disturbing them. This required the plotting of the trees and finding a space large enough for the main house and low-wood wings, while still maintaining a natural setting.

The principal portion of the castle was designed on two stories with a square, three-story tower having a pyramidal roof. A circular tower, two-stories high with a conical roof, is located opposite the square tower at the other end of the castle. Plans of the first floor contain the principal living quarters and the wings composed of a large living room, dining room, library, kitchens, several guest rooms, quarters for servants, caretakers, and other employees, and spacious garages. The second story, over the main castle structure, contains sleeping quarters with their baths, and a staircase giving access to the large, single room of the upper story of the square tower. All facilities were to be modern while still maintaining the atmosphere of an old Viking castle, an achievement admirably accomplished by the ingenious talents of the architect.

Excavation and foundations were begun in late August of 1928, and work was halted with the coming of early winter. As the castle was to be a faithful adaptation of an old castle in the days of the Vikings, the name Vikingsholm was appropriately chosen. The work resumed in the early spring of 1929. A large number of workmen were housed and fed in barracks constructed at the site. This was done in order to save time due to the brief season the men were able to work at Emerald Bay. Two Finnish carpenters were brought from the East in order that the wood hewing could be done by experienced men in an expert manner. Another craftsman woodcarver was found to enrich the structure with delicate carvings. Dark stone with contrasting white mortar was used, giving a striking effect similar to the stone castles of Southern Sweden. All timber used at Vikingsholm was of large dimensions similar to buildings built by the early Norsemen. On the principal portion of the castle, the first floor windows are rectangular and heavily mullioned, set in broad, shallow-arched openings of the stone walls. Upper windows of the square tower and both floors of the circular tower have smaller, rectangular windows varying in size but of an overall uniform design.

The castle's interior walls were lined with wide boards carefully dried and laid flat. Throughout the structure the wood is coated with a silvery grey water stain, sealed with banana oil, and finished in white wax. Located in some corners, with hearths traditionally raised fifteen inches from the floor, the Nordic fireplaces within the castle are authentic copies of those found in old Scandinavia. The fire screens are also of authentic design and inscription. The crown chimneys of Vikingsholm assume their name from their shape and originate from Dalecailia Province in Sweden.

On the second floor is a beautifully designed, projecting timber balcony. This was constructed in a similar manner to early wooden houses of the North Scandinavian countries, with corner posts fitted into the horizontal legs of the walls. The tracery of the windows blend well with the hand-carved design of the timbers, giving the balcony a medieval quaintness of Old-World charm.

Upon entering the courtyard one sees the right wing constructed of stone and roofed with growing sod with a sprinkler system, while the left wing is of wood with rough split logs, or pole timbers, covering the roof. The castle's nail-studded entrance door is sturdy and handsomely carved in a diamond pattern and fitted with ornate door hinges. The large, diamond-shaped glass side panels flanking this door are deeply casemented with carved, matching beam framing. In the main front entrance hall stands a life-size wooden figure that was hand-carved and clothed in the form of a Finnish peasant girl. This figure, constructed by the architect, has a circular clock built into the face. The figure was affectionately named Selma by Mrs. Knight and is similar to those found in Finland.

Passing through the hall in the main house gives access to the spacious living room with its panoramic view of Emerald Bay. Two detailed, carved beams with dragonhead endings hang from the ceilings, as did beams in the main room of houses of the Vikings after ceilings were added. Much of the handsome furniture in this room, as in others, are excellent replicas of fine museum pieces. Fine exhibits of suited armor pieces are also found in the rooms. A large, brick-lined fireplace occupies one corner of this room with a high mantel and ornate iron grillwork. The patterned ceiling and colorful cornice beams are well suited in creating an overall effect with the appropriate furnishings and handwoven Finnish wall hangings.

The dining room contains an original antique cupboard circa 1700, from Denmark. The table was made from a design by Palme to match the 1750 Danish antique chairs. The fireplace and carved, suspended lighting fixture support add to the authenticity of this interesting room. Most of the furniture on the second floor was made from drawings by Palme after eighteenth- and early nineteenth-century Swedish pieces from various museums. Within the third-story square tower room are twin, oak beds made to exact replicas of the queen's bed found in the famous Oslo Viking ship, but lengthened from its original four feet six inches. The lighting fixture in the round tower room was designed by the architect after a copy of an old butter mold, but with a new purpose. Several other interesting lighting fixtures throughout the castle were also designed by Palme.

The caretaker's house was also built in the Viking manner of logs. The roof of this building is overlaid with split logs fitted in a manner so that no spikes were used to hold them in place, but with a modern roof constructed under this as in the other log-covered wings. The boards making up the gutters are held in place by long pieces of wood, uniform in shape, with pointed ends. This type of construction dates from early times as a defense against unfriendly intruders.

Vikingsholm was completed in September of 1929 as a faithfully reproduced castle structure dating back some twelve hundred years. In addition to the main castle building there are several well-kept guest houses and buildings located throughout the grounds, including a boathouse, a summer house, garages, and stables. A steam plant was installed at the time the castle was erected, providing heat to each of the more than thirty rooms of the castle. One other modern convenience is a stainless-steel-equipped kitchen adjoining the dining room and butler's pantry.

Within Emerald Bay, not far from the shore, stands a small, secluded island, part of the Vikingsholm estate, known as Fannette Island. Upon its rugged, rocky summit, Mrs. Knight had a stone, single-room teahouse constructed that contains four small windows and a fireplace. This sixteen-foot-square structure affords solitude and a magnificent open view of Emerald Bay and the surrounding mountains. A boat channel, private lagoon, and extensive private beach are also a part of the beautiful estate grounds.

Mrs. Knight spent many happy years at Vikingsholm Castle, where she entertained friends amidst the peaceful beauty of this Lake Tahoe region. For many years she was a member of the Daughters of the American Revolution, at Santa Barbara, and a life member of the Massachusetts Society of Mayflower Descendents.

Mrs. Lora Josephine Knight died in 1945, leaving her magnificent Vikingsholm Castle as a true monument of ancient Scandinavian architecture. Vikingsholm is now preserved in Emerald Bay as a unique example complementary to the forceful scenery of the High Sierras and rugged spirit of the Vikings.

Vikingsholm Castle, placed among the stately trees of
the Emerald Bay area of Lake Tahoe, California.
*Courtesy State of California Department of Parks and
Recreation.*

Vikingsholm Castle, showing towers and wood balcony. *Courtesy South Lake Tahoe News Bureau.*

Sheer mountain walls rise as a background to Vikingsholm Castle. Stonework in the castle is uniform, contrasting to the low wings enclosing the courtyard. *Courtesy State of California Department of Parks and Recreation.*

An early photograph of Vikingsholm Castle, showing broad arches of window casements and stepping stone path to one of the entries. *Tavern Studio, Lake Tahoe, California, courtesy Mrs. Tara Stoke.*

Scandanavian constructed balcony at the second-story level adjoining the square, three story tower. *Courtesy Lennart Palme.*

The three-story square tower shows a variation in window design. Upper windows in this picture are covered. The pyramidal roof design contrasts to the conical roof of the round tower. *Courtesy South Lake Tahoe News Bureau.*

Courtyard of Vikingsholm Castle showing entrance door to the main castle building and service wing with sod roof. *Courtesy Lennart Palme.*

Main entrance drive through the caretaker's house leads to the courtyard. Walls show hand-hewn wood-work. *Courtesy South Lake Tahoe News Bureau.*

Upper portion of the caretaker's house spans the main entrance from the road. Along the gutters of the split log roof are pointed members used in early times as a defense against intruders. *Courtesy Lennart Palme.*

The utility wings of the main house show carved woodwork, crown chimney, and sod roof. *Courtesy Lennart Palme.*

Mrs. Lora J. Knight at the entrance door to the main house of Vikingsholm Castle. *Courtesy Mrs. Tara Stoke.*

The living room of Vikingsholm Castle displays much antique furniture amid the splendor of Viking architecture. The carved hanging beam depicts a dragon. *Courtesy State of California Department of Parks and Recreation.*

The dining room cupboard is an original antique from Denmark, ca. 1700. The table was made after a design by the architect to match the Danish antique chairs of 1750. *Courtesy State of California Department of Parks and Recreation.*

Lengthened from their original four feet, six inches, these replicas of the queen's bed found in a ship buried at Oslo some twelve hundred years ago are located in the third-story tower room. *Courtesy State of California Department of Parks and Recreation.*

This interior room shows patterned walls and interesting ceiling designs with a broad arched window opening. *Courtesy Mrs. Tara Stoke.*

Tower room library during the residence of Mrs. Lora
J. Knight. *Courtesy Mrs. Tara Stoke.*

A typical Nordic fireplace raised up from the floor. *Courtesy Lennart Palme.*

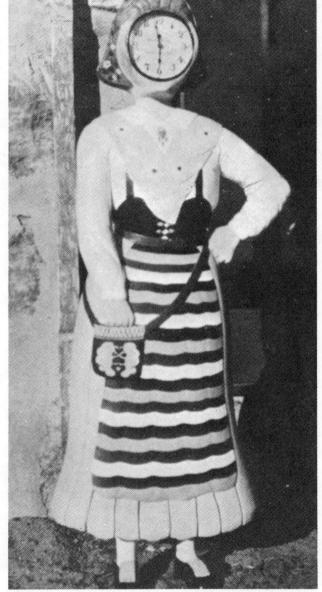

The life-size peasant clock is similar to those found in Finland. The architect made this clock for Mrs. Knight, who named it Selma. *Courtesy Lennart Palme.*

The teahouse atop rugged Fannette Island just offshore from the castle. A view of mountainous splendor awaits the visitor. *Courtesy South Lake Tahoe News Bureau.*

] 6 [
BOLDT CASTLE

GEORGE C. BOLDT, BORN ON THE PRUSSIAN ISLAND of Rugen in the Baltic Sea, on April 25, 1851, was the son of a merchant and educated in the common schools. At the age of thirteen he traveled alone to the United States, where he obtained employment in a New York hotel. With his savings he journeyed to Texas, where he ventured unsuccessfully in a chicken farm and sheep ranch. He later returned to New York and the hotel service, where he made massive advances from general utility man to steward in Parker's Restaurant in New York City.

From there he took a post as steward at the famous Clover Club in Philadelphia. It was here that influential members helped him establish a large, private residence into a hotel called the Bellevue. He won the gratitude of William Waldorf Astor for a favor, and when Astor decided to abandon his residence at Fifth Avenue and Thirty-Fourth Street, Boldt persuaded him to build the Waldorf Hotel on the site.

George Boldt was named manager of the Waldorf, which opened in 1893, then the most magnificent hotel in the world. At first, business was slow, and at one time, in August, it had only thirty-two guests, which caused speculation among other hotel men who saw it as a failure. But the Waldorf provided the best for people who demanded it, and within a few years Boldt had built up a great, flourishing business that made the hotel too small. By 1898 the Astoria was completed, forming the Waldorf-

Astoria, which Boldt made famous the world over and which was serviced by as many as fourteen hundred employees at its peak of business.

While continuing in the capacity of president of the Waldorf-Astoria Hotel Company, Boldt turned again to Philadelphia, where he bought the old Stratford adjoining the Bellevue. On the site he erected the new Bellevue-Stratford Hotel.

George Boldt married Louise Kehrer, of Philadelphia, and in the year 1900 he and his wife began visiting the Thousand Islands region of the St. Lawrence River, where they were much impressed with the beauties of the place. It was here that he bought Hart Island from George K. Hart. Hart had bought the island from Sisson and Fox, merchants of Alexandria Bay, who in turn had purchased the property from William McCue, who originally paid one hundred dollars for it. The Harts had built a wooden cottage on their island, and this is where Mr. and Mrs. Boldt spent their summers. George Boldt had decided on something special for this island retreat. This was to be the place where his youthful dream for a castle, like those he had seen on the Rhine River, was to emerge into a reality. The architectural firm of Hewitt, Stevens and Paist, of Philadelphia, was commissioned to do the work, with their client's word that expense was to be a minor consideration. Mr. and Mrs. Boldt furnished the ideas and real inspiration of the great project while the architects furnished the technical details with designs conforming to their clients' desires.

The best of workmen, landscape gardeners, electricians, artists, masons, and other highly skilled men in their fields came from all over the world to contribute their special talents and energy to this would-be magnificent structure. From Boldt's own quarries on Oak Island, ten miles away, many barges of granite were brought to the island site. And from his own sand pits tons of sand were hauled for the mixing of mortar. Terra-cotta was used as roofing for some of the buildings. Spotless white-marble mantelpieces, beautifully carved by Italian carftsmen, were brought over from Italy. Carvings, mosaics, sculpture, and tapestries arrived from the Old World to adorn this place of beauty. Numerous paintings from France, Germany, and Italy were purchased to decorate the walls.

Of the eleven buildings intended, the main castle building was to be the central point of the whole, being large enough to accommodate one hundred guest and their servants. The first and second floors contained the reception room, dining room, ballroom, library, and billiard rooms. The upper floors contained bedroom apartments, each with a private bath and an attractive brick fireplace. Exquisite tapestries and graceful chandeliers were purchased to adorn the walls of the grand marble tread staircase, which added to and completed a setting of royal splendor.

The first structure to be completed was the rugged, stone Alster Tower, fashioned after an ancient castle on the Rhine. Standing on the southeastern edge of the island, this structure was used by George Boldt as a summer residence while work continued on the main building. The tower could be approached from four sides, where heavy balustrades lined flights of stone steps. The basement of this tower is said to have contained a bowling alley, while plans of the upper floors called for the luxury of billiard room, library, café, and kitchen with bedrooms above. Because of the shape of the roof, the top floor was named the Shell Room, and was used for dancing. From the tower one could view the immediate surroundings in addition to a splendid panorama of the many lush islands of the area. The top of the square tower had a battlemented perimeter, and several windows were built into the tower sides on all levels with stone balcony and porches at the lower levels.

Close by the Alster Tower is the stone-arched water gate that leads to the lagoon from which little waterways surround nearly half the island. Bordering the lagoon on the outside is a long embankment used as a promenade.

At the eastern end of the island is the beautifully designed medieval tower that was intended as a powerhouse generating plant to provide the necessary power for the estate and to illuminate the grounds. The upper floors of the powerhouse were intended for engineers' and mechanics' lodgings. The servants were to be housed in a separate building with recreation facilities for all. In this area is the medieval clock and chimes tower building. This charming little structure is like an independent island castle with access from the main island by a quaint stone, arched bridge. Small conical roofs cap the circular towers and, with the main clock tower, join the corners of the central two-story building that also had a third-story attic within the roof. The roofs of most of these smaller structures are no longer existing. The island itself had a natural covering of mass shrubbery with rocky shores that were blended into the setting of the island's landscape. This shore was reworked so as to resemble the shape of a heart from which the island derived its name, and it is often referred to as Heart Island. Provisions were made for a swan pond at the western end of the island, while a smaller fish pond was constructed at the southern end. On an elevated rock plateau, landscape gardeners laid out the Italian gardens at one side of the main castle building.

As a scene of beauty itself, the castle had been placed in a setting worthy of its noble character. The stonework of the main building is less rugged in appearance compared to some of the other surrounding structures. Passing through the foyer, the main great hall was reached, from which rose the grand staircase to the floors above. Next to the library on the main floor was the main drawing room, where a recess for a pipe organ and chime-controlled keyboard were to be located for the sounding of the Westminister chimes located in the powerhouse. Also on this floor was the dining room in addition to butler's pantries and storerooms. The kitchens were located in the basement with facilities connecting the serving areas above.

The second floor contained the master suite of rooms intended to be occupied by Mr. and Mrs. Boldt. Also on this floor were the guest rooms, as were on the third and fourth floors above. A short flight of stairs led to the top-floor lookout where the Thousand Islands and St. Lawrence River could be seen in a breathtaking panoramic view.

In the basement, with an entrance under the grand staircase, was the swimming pool with lounge and adjacent dressing rooms and additional lounging rooms. Located in other rooms were the heating systems and a tramway tunnel intended for transporting supplies from the water's edge.

Two years had passed since the work had begun. The army of workmen had not overlooked any of the painstaking detail called for in this monumental work of architecture that was to be a gift to George Boldt's beloved wife. While nearing completion in mid-January, a telegram was sent to the superintendent of construction to stop work on the castle. The fateful day of this magnificent structure of more than ninety rooms had come, for the main castle building would never be completed. Mrs. Boldt was dead. What had begun as a glorious work of architecture was now subject to the fate of a ruin as workmen departed and the castle was abandoned.

This admirable structure with its quaint surrounding buildings that comprised so much planning, work, and hope was now left to the mercy of time and the elements. As the years passed no attempt was made to continue the work of completing the castle. Weeds grew where the great ballroom was planned, and birds built their nests in the empty towers. On December 5, 1916, George Boldt died at the age of sixty-five. Older people recalled Boldt as a man with an agreeable Prussian accent and with a simple and pleasant personality.

The castle was sold in 1918 to millionaire Edward J. Noble, who never intended to occupy the property but opened it to the public. Thousands of tourists visited the castle, arriving by boats to new piers constructed for them. On the evening of August 9, 1936 the roof of the quaint clock tower was destroyed by fire caused by aerial fireworks in connection with weekend entertainment on the island. After Noble's death in 1959, his heirs kept the castle open to the public until 1962, when the Treadway Corporation took over its operation as a tourist attraction.

Much of the construction has been destroyed through neglect and vandalism. Today the Boldt Castle stands as a ruined shell, a curiosity for the visitor who may only imagine what grandeur it might have had. Now only a silent memory remains, a skeleton of the dream George Boldt had of a castle with lofty turrets and a majestic setting typifying an era long since past.

Hart Island, among the Thousand Islands of Alexandria Bay, New York. The main castle building, the Alster Tower, and a portion of the powerhouse can be seen in this aerial photo. Lower left shows the water gate. *Courtesy New York State Department of Commerce.*

Aerial photo shows Boldt Castle as it exists today. Foliage has grown inside the walls of several of the buildings as seen in the powerhouse in the lower right corner of the picture. *Roger L. Moore, courtesy New York State Department of Commerce.*

Boldt Castle in winter. The shape of Hart Island is clearly defined in this photo. *Courtesy Staff Photograph, Watertown Daily Times, Watertown, New York.*

A portion of the clock-and-chimes tower as it appears today. The roofs and clock have long disappeared. *Roger L. Moore, courtesy New York State Department of Commerce.*

Boldt Castle's main building showing closeup of stonework. Note the animal figure on the upper right roof.
*Roger L. Moore, courtesy New York State Depart-
ment of Commerce.*

Boldt Castle on Hart Island is now a popular tourist attraction. Privately owned sailing craft often circle the island castle for an overall view. *Courtesy Treadway Thousand Islands Club.*

View of Hart Island in Alexandria Bay, New York. Service docks are seen in the foreground. *Reproduced from the collections of the Library of Congress.*

Hart Island is open to tourists from May to October. The main Castle building is seen in the background surrounded by the island's many trees. *Staff Photograph, courtesy Watertown Daily Times, Watertown, New York.*

This powerhouse once supplied electricity to the other structures on Hart Island. The clock-and-chimes tower is also seen with other islands in the background. The arched bridge is the only access to the main island, since this structure is surrounded by water. *Reproduced from the collections of the Library of Congress.*

The rugged Alster Tower on Hart Island. Boldt spent his summers here while work continued in the main building and other structures on the island. *Reproduced from the collections of the Library of Congress.*

The stone, arched water gate as it appears today, with a portion of the swan pond in the foreground. Alster Tower is seen in the background. *Roger L. Moore, courtesy New York State Department of Commerce.*

] 7 [
STAUNTON HILL

LOCATED IN CHARLOTTE COUNTY, VIRGINIA, THE Staunton Hill estate was founded by James Bruce in 1801 with the purchase of 682 acres of land between the Blue Ridge Mountains and the Staunton River. Having been owner of a system of chain stores and other properties, James Bruce was considered one of America's wealthiest men when he died in 1839.

One of his two sons, Charles Bruce, a graduate of Harvard College, inherited the acres in Charlotte County where he was to erect a structure that became one of America's fine examples of Gothic revival architecture. Prior to embarking on a grand tour of Europe in 1848, Bruce commissioned his friend, architect John E. Johnson, to design and build a structure appropriate to the estate because the original house was inadequate and unsuited to the property. Bruce was engaged to Sarah Seddon, and upon his return from Europe they planned to marry and live in the new country residence. Over the years the estate grounds increased, amounting to over five thousand acres with the additional purchases.

Due to the remote site of construction, workmen were brought in from Philadelphia to build the crenellated structure with its many turrets and grey marble portico. As with the portico, marble for the pillars, flooring, and fireplace mantels came from Italy to Philadelphia, where it was crafted to its purpose and then sent by boat to the estate's landing docks.

Construction was completed in 1850, resulting in a sturdy and most picturesque castellated structure built of bricks with a stucco surface enclosing fourteen large rooms. The building's central portion contains three stories with adjacent wings on either side, each two stories high. A conservatory had once connected to the main building but was destroyed many years ago. The road leading to the circular drive entrance court is now flanked at the gate by a pair of identical sculptured hounds resting on brick bases. In addition to the well-kept garden paths, lawns, and native trees, the landscaping is further enhanced with rare shrubs and numerous trees imported from foreign lands.

The portico is constructed of excellent blue-grey marble supported by slender quatrefoil columns that meet at the extremities of shallow Tudor arches. The ceiling has a multivaulted design, and with its crenellated, two-level roof perimeter the overall effect of the portico hints of a delicate cloister appearance.

Window designs vary with plain, rectangular framing, Gothic, oriel, and bay windows, in addition to the use of stained glass. An indication of window variety is found on the second and third stories above the portico and the first-floor windows of this facade. In the central building portion the windows are of Gothic design with heavy mullions enclosing long, slender panes, while flanking windows of the second floor are rectangular, but display tracery in the upper window portions.

Several octagonal turrets located at the four corners of the three-story central portion rise up from their bases at the building foundation and extend a few feet above the third-story roof. Also extending above the roof are several chimney shafts, each topped by clusters of smokestacks, all of similar design, giving an indication of the numerous fireplaces within. Evenly spaced merlons that highlight and blend well with the turrets and chimney shafts are found on the second- and third-floor roof perimeter.

Though Staunton Hill presents aspects of a medieval castellated structure in its outward appearance, the interior is surprisingly rewarding in the contrasting warmth and variations of ornate Gothic style. The principal rooms of the first floor are the drawing room, called the sun-room, middle drawing room, large dining room, library, stair hall, and octagonal hall. Spacious bedrooms occupy the second floor, one of which has a small, diamond-paned oriel window. The third-floor tower room occupies the entire floor and features the large, deep-casemented Gothic window.

The octagonal hall, located at one end of the central building, has four doorways that provide access to the portico and opposite stair hall in addition to the sun-room and dining room at opposite wings. Between the doorways are four arched niches containing pedestaled, sculptured figures. The floor is patterned in neat rows of black and white marble tiles. A low, marble baseboard surrounds the hall walls with a frieze terminating at the upper walls. The octagonal, shallow-arched ceiling is spaced by ribs that radiate from the ceiling's center, ending at the upper wall corners above the frieze. Terrace entry doors are framed with side and upper panels in beautiful stained-glass designs set deep in Gothic moldings.

Adjoining the octagonal hall is the stair hall with its beautifully designed twin staircases. Located on opposite walls, the stairs curve at their bases and again at an upper landing where they meet to form a short, central flight to the second floor. The landing also forms a small part of the stair hall ceiling that meets with and follows the curvature of the stairs to their bases. Leading up from exquisite mahogany newels, wide mahogany rails are supported by numerous slender balusters connected at the rail by a series of small, wood arches that span each balustrade.

The east door of the octagonal hall leads to the spacious dining room where Charles Bruce lavishly entertained his guests with fine foods and drink. The lower walls have a square-paneled, carved wainscot, while a frieze borders the high upper walls. Doorways have heavy, wood-designed moldings, as does the fireplace mantel with its carved-wood hunting scene. The fireplace opening is framed in a broad band of marble with wood side paneling extending up from the floor and above the mantel, enclosing the chimney piece up to the frieze. Framed glass doors open to the terrace similar to those of the sun-room in the opposite wing.

The sun-room, located from the west door of the octagonal hall, has its high ceiling similar in design to the middle drawing room. The cornice is intricately designed in a patterned series of trefoils, cusps, and tiny arches that fan out to form pointed arches. The sun-room's frieze and cornice are similar to those of the middle drawing room and library, with plaster molding ceiling identical to that of the middle drawing room. Imported from Venice, Gothic mirrors of identical design hang on opposite walls with the base of one mirror frame resting on the fireplace mantel. The marble fireplaces of the sun-room and middle room are identical to Tudor arched openings and mantels.

Broad, graceful archways adjoin the middle room at each end with pairs of sliding doors spaced within the common, connecting walls. This arch and sliding door arrangement of the sun-room, middle room, and library provided a simultaneous view of all three rooms when the doors are opened. Tudor arched bay windows flank the fireplace of the middle room, which also contains two Gothic mirrors matching those of the sun-room and placed in similar locations.

The library ceiling is of the same height as the connecting two rooms but of a rectangular, paneled pattern. The marble fireplace is also of similar design with all three chimney pieces on the same wall face. A bay window with leaded glass sash faces the court. Shallow, pointed arches span the built-in bookcases and doorway, all having wooden crenellated members over the arches. The ends of the door and bookcase arches rest on clusters of slender, triple colonnettes, which are of similar design to the bay window mullions in this room.

In the early 1860s, when the clouds of war broke

out, Charles Bruce organized and equipped, at his own expense, the Staunton Hill Artillery. As captain, he rode off with his company in 1862, a proud and noble man faced with the possibility of never returning to his family and the wonderful years at Staunton Hill.

During her husband's absence, Mrs. Bruce was left in charge of the vast estate. Federal troops were advancing in the direction of Staunton Hill, and in her anxiety to retain the silver and other old family treasures from their grasp she had them buried in a dense woodland some distance away. But the troops did not come to the mansion since it was beyond their path of travel. By odd coincidence the troops camped on the very site that Mrs. Bruce had carefully chosen to bury the family treasure. Fortunately, the camp was soon vacated with the troops moving on without their knowledge of the wealth hidden beneath them.

After Charles Bruce returned to his home he was later able to serve three terms as a member of the Virginia State Senate. Not seeking the offered nomination to Congress, Bruce spent his time with the enormous task of keeping up the vast estate with its fields of grain, tobacco, and surrounding buildings.

Charles Bruce died in 1896, and the estate was divided among his four children. This magnificent structure survives today and is still privately owned by a member of the Bruce family. With lofty turrets of Old-World charm the battlemented architecture of Staunton Hill leaves America with a treasure of Gothic revival, a distinction in its class, and a reminder of classic country life in days gone by.

Staunton Hill, Charlotte County, Virginia, 1848. *Courtesy Virginia State Library.*

Entrance to Staunton Hill with circular drive. *Courtesy Virginia Museum of Fine Arts.*

Staunton Hill, from an old photograph. *Courtesy Virginia State Library.*

Main entrance of Staunton Hill with circular drive to entry. *Courtesy Virginia State Library.*

Marble portico with clustered columns and portion of
base of one of the high towers. *Courtesy Virginia
Museum of Fine Arts.*

Marble portico showing detail of the ceiling. *Courtesy Virginia State Library.*

Detail showing diamond-paned bay window and typical chimney piece. *Courtesy Virginia State Library.*

Beautifully designed twin staircases of the stair hall
lead to the upper floor. The paired gilt mirrors were
especially made in Venice. *Courtesy Virginia Museum
of Fine Arts.*

The octagonal hall displays classical figures in niches around the walls. Floors are patterned in marble. *Courtesy Virginia Museum of Fine Arts.*

The terrace doors are framed with stained-glass panels. *Courtesy Virginia Museum of Fine Arts.*

Georgian dining room with marble fireplace and wood-paneled chimney piece. *Courtesy Virginia Museum of Fine Arts.*

Drawing room. Matching mirrors are also found in
the adjoining drawing room. *Courtesy Virginia Museum
of Fine Arts.*

Gothic design of the library with crenellated bookcases and doorways is well adapted in this beautiful
room. *Courtesy Virginia Museum of Fine Arts.*

] 8 [

GILLETTE CASTLE

WILLIAM HOOKER GILLETTE, EMINENT ACTOR AND playwright, was born on July 24, 1853, in Hartford, Connecticut, where he received his early education. His parental families were pioneering Americans noted in Connecticut with service to Connecticut history. His father, Francis Gillette, became a United States senator and was a very prominent figure in establishing the present Republican party. William Gillette's mother was a direct descendant of one of the founders of the city of Hartford, Reverend Thomas Hooker.

In 1882 William Gillette married Helen Nickels of Detroit and, after a brief span of only six years, he was widowed, never to remarry again. As an actor, Gillette worked very hard, appearing in various stock companies for a number of years and playing leading roles in many of his own dramas. He is credited in creating thirteen original plays and seven adaptations, upon two of which he collaborated. Among these plays were *The Professor,* 1881; *The Private Secretary,* 1884; *Held by the Enemy,* 1886; *Secret Service,* 1895; and *Sherlock Holmes,* 1899. Gillette's portrayal of Conan Doyle's famous detective, Sherlock Holmes, became legendary with more than thirteen hundred performances spanning over thirty years, from 1899 to 1932. Though Gillette's play had little to do with the Holmes tales, his characterization of Sherlock Holmes, the costume of the hunting cap, the Inverness cape, and the pipe were originally established by Gillette and adapted by other artists illustrating Sherlock Holmes in later tales. Through his efforts in the portrayal, as he became known to millions of people throughout the world, William Gillette became established in the public mind as the master detective, giving life and substance to the famous fictional character. Gillette's lifetime income from the theater and royalties from his plays amounted to over three million dollars, at a time when there were no income tax deductions and a dollar held its true value.

By 1912, while at the height of his career, Gillette decided to build a home and settle down. Several sites were explored, with a location near Greenport, Long Island, being his choice. While on a leisurely cruise up the Connecticut River in his houseboat, the *Aunt Polly,* he was greatly impressed with the striking, tree-filled terrain of the area and anchored his craft for an overnight stay on the east bank close to the Chester-Hadlyme ferry slip. The following morning he climbed to the summit of the southmost and highest of seven hills known as the Seven Sisters. High above the water's edge he was rewarded by the overwhelming view. The Long Island homesite was soon replaced with this magnificent location, and within a short time he purchased one hundred and fifteen acres of this land that gave him three quarters of a mile of shoreline and good depth.

Gillette's previous plans for a rambling summer home were discarded in favor of a castellated-type stone structure. The hill was composed of solid rock and virgin forests, and the high altitude without easy access posed a serious problem of getting the needed construction materials up to the site. Gillette's inventive ability led him to devise and construct an aerial, cabled tramway that was used to transport workmen and building materials from the dock below up to the summit of the hill.

Gillette designed the plans and details for the entire castle and undertook the supervision of construction, which was done by the Hartford contracting builder, Porteus-Walker Company. In 1914 work was begun on building roads, clearing the site, hauling materials, and constructing the castle's foundation. Being built on solid granite rock, the basement was carved into this natural formation by drilling and blasting out the rock to a depth of over twelve feet. The entire castle is constructed of native granite obtained from the area around the site. At their base, the foundation walls are five feet thick, gradually decreasing upward to the two-foot thickness of the towers. Various walks are also carved out from the solid rock of the high cliffs and bordered by low, stone walls. Because of the nature of the construction involved, twenty-two skilled masons worked on the entire structure for several years.

Gillette called his great stone creation the Seventh Sister, but it is more popularly known as the Gillette Castle. The castle, patterned after a medieval Rhennish fortress, was sufficiently completed in 1919 for Gilette to take up residence there after five years of continuous construction. The total investment of Gillette's Castle is not recorded, but estimates have it at over one million dollars, not counting the additional thousands he invested on his whims of altering and adding to the castle estate.

The outward appearance of the castle is one of a solid ruggedness, uniform in its stonework with a great number of windows capped by protruding icicle-shaped pendants. Small apertures, battlements, stone balconies, irregular exterior walls, and towers all add to this massive monument, unique in its architectural design and construction. The diamond-shaped windows of the upper floors contrast with the rectangular and square glass of the lower-floor windows. A great stone portico fronts the entry, which leads to an intriguing medieval-style oak door that opens to the main entrance hall. This entry door is one of assured security with its complex of latches, bars, and locking devices that would bewilder and

dismay any trespasser.

During the years Gillette occupied the castle he enjoyed adding and furnishing twenty-four rooms to the buildings. Numerous unusual features are found throughout the entire structure, many of which are unique and testify to Gillette's talent for inventiveness. He evidently had a flair for gadgets, such as the great number of locks and bolts found on some of the furniture and the forty-seven doors of the castle. His ingenuity is also evident in the unusual railroad-style wood-handle light switches, window fastenings, and many other mechanical devices. Another notable feature is the hanging wall suspended from steel beams without any support from the main floor.

Some of the more interesting rooms of the castle include the main living room, dining room, cocktail lounge, library, Gillette's bedroom, and private study. The spacious living room is walled in fieldstone, with a staircase at one end leading to a long balcony that encloses two of the walls and gives access to the rooms above. Stone columns support heavy oak beams that span the nineteen-foot-high braced ceiling. Opposite one of the balconies in this fifty-by-thirty-foot room is a large, fieldstone fireplace with its irregular mantle of the same material. Portions of the lower walls are paneled with squares of woven mats made to his order, with different colors blending in a pattern around the room. Much of the timber in this room, such as beams, bracing posts, door moldings, and other trimmings, have a hand-adzed finish that blends well with the rugged stone of the room. This adzed dressing of the wood is also found in various other rooms of the castle, both in the trim and in some of the furniture. The use of white oak and woven mats has much influence in several rooms that illustrate Gillette's preference for this material.

Near the living room is a large conservatory with its long, paneled-glass walls and profusion of planted greenery. A pool built into the floor is surrounded by large rocks at varying elevations with waterfalls cascading into the pond where Gillette once kept varieties of rare goldfish and two pet frogs, Lena and Mike. The various plants and shrubs blend well against stone columns bracing the skylighted ceiling and enclosed, framed-glass walls of this spacious conservatory.

Though Gillette was a gracious host, his guests

were usually limited to very close friends, thus a large dining room was not necessary. As a result the dining room is small, perhaps moreso than might be expected in such a large structure. It was nevertheless quite suitable for him and not lacking in his taste for unusual features. The dining table operates on metal rollers on a track that lock in place when guests roll it toward them after being seated on the wall bench. Facing the fireplace, Gillette usually sat in the center of the cushioned bench and could ring for the butler by pressing a certain floorboard under the table that had an electrical control connected with the butler's pantry. At one end of the dining room is a pair of massive sliding doors with intricate locks. The wood of this door frame is adzed, as are other built-in furnishings in this area.

Next to the living room, and in a corner nearest the dining room, is the cocktail lounge with its matted walls and unique bar, installed in 1934. The bar is a showpiece of unusual cabinet work, which Gillette usually kept well-stocked for his guests. The bar contains a special locking device controlled by a pressure panel on the rear of the cabinet that not only automatically opens the bar but also turns on the bar lights.

At the far end of the cocktail lounge is Gillette's study, with its adzed beam ceiling and matted walls. This room is virtually untouched and as Gillette left it with the exception of a few minor personal items that were removed after his death. His desk, with its intricate locking device, is the same one he used when writing many of his famous plays. There is much interesting furniture in this room, including an armchair fitted with metal rollers that moves on a wood track. A concealed doorway on a wall behind this chair leads to the main entrance hall, providing quick access to the outside of the castle.

The art gallery is located on the fourth floor and once contained over one hundred paintings, consisting mostly of pastoral scenes and seascapes. The library is also located on this floor.

Gillette's bedroom is small but contains a well-concealed bath and numerous gadgets built for his comfort. The upper half of the walls are of wood, with squares of matting covering the lower portion. Some of the hand-carved furniture is of interesting design, in contrast to the plain bed made of white, enameled iron. These white, iron beds are a common feature in the other bedrooms, which all vary in dimension from one another.

A hanging lever located in the living room at one end of the balcony was installed connecting to a system that provided water in case of a fire. A fresh-water spring near the castle was available to provide water for drinking and other domestic uses.

Besides adding the many unique devices, furniture, and other features to the castle over the years, Gillette found time to indulge in many hobbies during his long life. From 1901 he kept his houseboat, the *Aunt Polly,* as a second home. It was well outfitted and equipped with such rooms as a library, lounge, salon, and sleeping quarters. It had a nineteen-foot beam with a top speed of ten knots and carried a crew of eight. In 1903 a forty-foot section was added to increase living space, giving a total length of 140 feet. Boating cruises included trips along the inland waters of the Atlantic coast, which he continued to take in his later years. In 1932 a fire destroyed the houseboat, which was docked below the castle, thus ending forever the unforgettable sailing days of the aged actor.

In earlier years Gillette was an enthusiastic motor-cyclist with a craving for speed. His topping seventy miles an hour accounted for his frequent trips to the County Court in Middlesex, where the authorities tried to acquaint him with the speed limits of the area. Another hobby he enjoyed immensely was large-scale model trains, especially locomotives. After completion of the castle in 1919, Gillette began constructing the Seventh Sister Shortline, a narrow-gauge railway system spread about his property that accommodated several pieces of rolling stock, including two locomotives. One of these locomotives was powered by steam, the other by electricity. These engines, along with two Pullmans and an observation car, were made to Gillette's specifications and ran on three miles of track with its turnouts, trestles, stations, and roundhouse.

Gillette's yearning for speed never left him even in his later years, when he invited his guests to ride in the cars of the train while he operated the engine. Though only able to obtain twenty miles an hour, he delighted in operating his iron horse, blasting the engine's whistle and speeding around curves at full throttle without regard to the hand brakes or the shattered nerves of his passengers. Fortunately no accidents occurred during those years the private railroad was operating. The estimated fifty thousand dollars worth of equipment and tracks are no longer at the castle, since they were purchased for three thousand dollars by an amusement park at Lake Compounce after Gillette passed away.

Another enjoyment of Gillette's was that of his pet cats, which at one time amounted to seventeen. Evidence of his liking for these animals is found in the castle, where over seventy objects of various cat images, made of different materials, are located about the many rooms.

Gillette maintained a happy household during his lifetime at the castle. He enjoyed the music of his favorite composer, Chopin, and heard selections that suited his mood played on the player piano located in the living room. In 1913 Gillette was elected to membership in the National Institute of Arts and Letters and was chosen as one of fifty Immortals by this organization. In recognition for his work as a dramatist, this institute honored him again in 1931 with a gold medal, and in 1933 his portrait received an honored place on the wall of the American Academy of Arts and Letters. He was also a member of other noted associations and held honorary degrees from various colleges, including Columbia University.

William Gillette died on April 29, 1937, at the age of eighty-four and is buried near his wife in a wooded cemetery in Farmington, Connecticut. Before he died, Gillette had been worried about the future of his cherished castle creation. As a result of his concern he left provisions in his will that the executor of his estate not let the property come into the possession "of some blithering saphead who has no conception of where he is or with what surrounded."

In 1943 the castle was acquired by the Connecticut State Park and Forest Commission and is opened to the public for several months during the year. Thousands of people visit the Gillette Castle State Park annually to wander through the many intriguing rooms and leisurely stroll about the gardens, perhaps to look out on the magnificent panoramic view of the broad Connecticut River stretching for miles to the distant hills. The Gillette Castle is still the sturdy structure it was years ago when the famous figure of the American stage first conceived this enduring sentinal high upon the wooded hill.

William Gillette in his early years. *Ray Mainwaring, courtesy Connecticut State Park and Forest Commission.*

Gillette Castle, showing portion of main entrance. The rough stone exterior is clearly shown in this picture with balconies and battlements of similar architectural design. *Courtesy Ray Mainwaring*.

Exterior corner of the castle showing its rugged architecture and various window designs. *Courtesy Ray Mainwaring*.

Exterior of Gillette Castle with its rugged stonework and icicle-shaped pendants. *Courtesy Ray Mainwaring.*

The living room in Gillette Castle shows adzed beams, furniture, and other woodwork that displays this finish. *Courtesy Ray Mainwaring.*

The great fireplace in the living room displays cat ornaments, Gillette's favorite animal. The adzed woodwork in the stair railing is typical throughout the castle. *Courtesy Ray Mainwaring.*

Gillette's interesting bar is seen through the living room doorway. The woven-mat walls and adzed timber are clearly shown. *Courtesy Ray Mainwaring.*

This table travels on a track. The background shows part of the conservatory with its glass wall. *Courtesy Ray Mainwaring.*

One of the massive doors in the dining room with its intricate locks. Note the adzed framing and mat walls. *Courtesy Ray Mainwaring.*

William Gillette's bedroom with mat walls and plain white enamel bed. This type of bed is found in other bedrooms of the castle. *Courtesy Ray Mainwaring.*

William Gillette's study, showing his desk with its
secret compartments and roll-back chair. The square
mats on the wall are also found throughout the castle.
Courtesy Ray Mainwaring.

] 9 [
LYNDHURST

LOCATED ON A WOODED HILLTOP ABOVE THE HUDson River at Tarrytown, New York, is one of America's finest examples of Gothic revival architecture, known as Lyndhurst. The evolution of this magnificent thirty-room stone-and-marble structure and its other buildings is actually the work of three families who occupied the estate that had its beginning in 1838. The original structure was designed for General William Paulding and his son Philip, by the renowned architect Alexander Jackson Davis, who also designed some fifty excellent pieces of furniture for Lyndhurst, much of which still occupies the building. Davis, who was also an artist and lithographer before becoming an architect, designed the dwelling as a summer retreat for the Pauldings at the time when many such buildings of the same period were quickly disappearing.

Born in 1770, General Paulding was near seventy when he and his son Philip, mayor of New York 1824–26, ventured into the building of what was then variously called Paulding's Manor, Paulding's Villa, The Knoll, and by their political opponets, Paulding's Folly. The structure, which was nearing its completion in 1842, was not a large building but occupied the greater southerly half of the main structure as we see it today. Built of Sing Sing Marble, the original architecture had a basement, main floor, second floor, and attic, in addition to a fine carriage entrance porch fronting a central hall lobby. There were also towers, turrets, buttresses,

bays, trefoils, pinnacled roofs, and windows incorporating heavy mullions and tracery. The main floor boasted a large drawing room and dining room, while the second floor was divided into chambers, one of which was Paulding's library, now a splendid art gallery. A most notable feature of the principal chambers are the detailed ceilings of rib vaulting or haunched beams carried on corbels.

In addition to the interior details are the variety of beautiful glass windows, mantels, door trim, parquetry floors, and a lovely over-the-mantel mirror in the reception room. While the work continued, business contracts with Davis were maintained by Philip Paulding. Their correspondence reflects a friendly relationship while attending to the details of construction.

General Paulding died in 1854, and in 1864 the estate was sold by his heirs to George Merrit, a New York City dry-goods merchant who named his newly acquired property Lyndhurst. Merrit decided to enlarge the building, which he found too small for his family, and engaged the same architect, Davis, to make the additions. Fortunately, Merrit retained the style of architecture while nearly doubling its size, thus creating an effect resulting in what we see today as a refined and modest castellated Gothic structure equal in elegance to any similar structure in England.

The once-small villa of General Paulding was now expanded with an added north wing and a great square tower that joined the old with the new. This addition was boldly executed by Davis, who achieved a harmonious transition of unified composition in the Gothic revival manner. The principal addition was a handsome, all-wood-ceilinged dining room and a vaulted-ceilinged bedroom above, both located north of the new tower. The original east carriage entrance lobby was enclosed in glass, and a new porte cochere was constructed directly opposite on the west face. The new four-storied tower, topped with battlements, was given various window designs and openings on each floor, the second of which was fronted by a beautifully designed and detailed oriel window. The porch originally on the south and west sides was extended to the east, and ornate chimney places were added, as was more Gothic revival furniture.

In addition to the expansion and remodeling of the main building, Merrit was now to give his attention to the grounds of the estate, which were to undergo a significant change. With advice given by the eminent horticulturist Andrew Downing about the development of the grounds, a crew of men were employed to start the work.

From their natural, wild state of undergrowth, meadows, swamps, and briars, the land was drained and converted into a beautiful park comprising some twenty acres in lawns, planted trees, shrubs, and a large grape arbor. Various fruit trees were planted bordering a vegetable garden in another portion of the grounds. A spacious stable built of marble, a coachman's lodge, gardener's quarters, and gate houses were also constructed. In addition, a vast, Oriental-style greenhouse, the largest in the United States, was also erected. The central portion of this greenhouse was eighty feet long by forty-six feet wide, and from the center rose a tower of one hundred feet high topped with a twenty-five-foot-diameter glass cupola. Stretching out on opposite sides of the tower were two long wings totaling some four hundred feet in length and terminated at the ends with wings each eighty feet long and thirty feet wide. To further add to the capacity of this structure a cellar ran underneath the entire greenhouse that housed water tanks, boiler rooms, coal rooms, and storage rooms for various materials and garden tools. The greenhouse was well kept and stocked by Merrit until his death in 1873, after which the plants were sold, the greenhouse fell to neglect, and the estate was offered for sale.

Lyndhurst was purchased in the spring of 1880 by Jay Gould and was to remain with the Gould family for the next eighty-four years. In early December of 1880, the recently restocked greenhouse was discovered in flames, which quickly spread, destroying the magnificent structure. The original builders of the greenhouse were soon called to rebuild a new greenhouse on the site, which was built similar in dimension but somewhat different in design to the previous structure. In place of the central tower and cupola, a large, circular dome was built, and the entire structure was restocked with numerous choice plants from various countries.

Jay Gould was born in 1836 in Rexburg, New York. After a hard and varied youth, and after having been hired by various employers, he found himself on Wall Street trading in railroad securities at the time of the Civil War. By the time he purchased Lyndhurst he controlled the Union Pacific Railroad and, later, Western Union Telegraph. Gould's reputation in financial transactions was anything but creditable according to those who had dealings with him. He was said to have been an unscrupulous robber baron who dealt ruthlessly in manipulating stocks, creating panics and false rumors, influencing judges and legislators to his own ends, and causing bankruptcy for many, and was accused of numerous other highly critical charges that resulted in many millions in profits for him. His daring transactions also caused the creation of many laws that now protect investors from such dealings known in Gould's time.

In great contrast to this side of Gould's character, recent revelations indicate that he anonymously performed worthy acts such as donating land to the Mount Vernon Ladies Association, which was trying to salvage the old plantation of George Washington at Mount Vernon, Virginia. Gould's life with his family reveals him as an entirely different person than as he was known on Wall Street. His reputation as a tough man of finance is nonexistent here where he is a loving father who enjoyed the company of his children, flowers, and good books. His dealings in finance were not always to his benefit. In 1884 he lost control of the Union Pacific, and a general decline in health, crippled by tuberculosis, caused him to spend his remaining years at Lyndhurst convalescing.

During the Gould ownership, no significant

changes were made on the exterior of the main building. A few interior additions were made that included electric lighting, a small elevator, extra bathrooms, and a heating plant. The kitchens were in the basement and connected with service facilities to the dining room by means of dumbwaiters that transported the food.

Gould was fifty-six years of age when he died, leaving Lyndhurst to his eldest daughter, Helen, who was his heir. Helen Gould was noted for her good works, which were her main interest, in addition to initiating millions of dollars of the Gould family wealth as donations to various institutions. She was awarded a gold medal by Congress for her personal efforts and work among the sick and wounded during the Spanish-American War. She delighted in being with children and held sewing classes and fresh-air parties for them on the grounds at Lyndhurst.

After her death in 1938, her younger sister, Anna, who had become Duchess of Talleyrand-Perigord, through marriage in 1908, moved from France to take possession of Lyndhurst. During World War II service men were entertained at the amply staffed estate. Though her life changed little at Lyndhurst, Anna maintained the house and grounds in excellent condition. All repairs to the principal buildings were made with instructions that new work was to be made identical to the original. Her remaining years were devoted to the maintenance of her family place until her death in 1961.

In November, 1964, the National Trust for Historic Preservation took possession of Lyndhurst with its interior treasures and sixty-seven acres of surrounding property. The estate is now open to the public as a nonprofit museum, existing in excellent condition as one of the finest Gothic revival structures in the United States.

Two south and east elevation sketches for Lyndhurst by A. J. Davis. *Courtesy the Metropolitan Museum of Art, Harris Brisbane Dick Fund, 1924.*

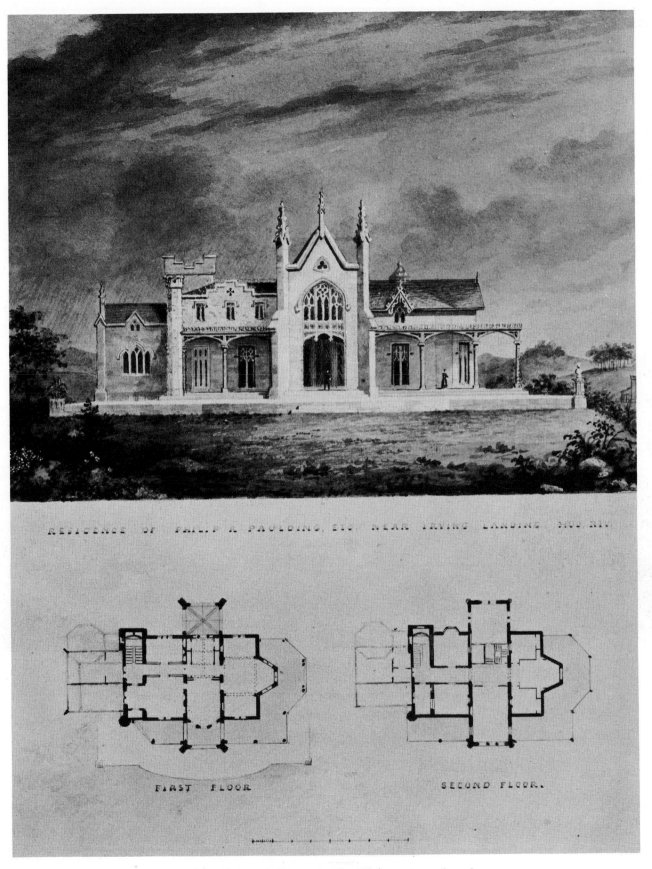

RESIDENCE OF PHILIP R. PAULDING, ESQ. NEAR IRVING LANDING. SING SING

FIRST FLOOR   SECOND FLOOR.

Drawing by A. J. Davis for Lyndhurst, west elevation
and two plans. *Courtesy the Metropolitan Museum of
Art, Harris Brisbane Dick Fund, 1924.*

Drawing by Davis of the west front, as enlarged for
Merritt. *Courtesy the Metropolitan Museum of Art,
Harris Brisbane Dick Fund, 1924.*

Drawing by Davis of Paulding dining room, 1837. *Courtesy the Metropolitan Museum of Art, Harris Brisbane Dick Fund, 1924.*

Drawing by Davis of oriel window. *Courtesy the Metropolitan Museum of Art, Harris Brisbane Dick Fund, 1924.*

The Merritt reception room. *Courtesy the collection of Mrs. Alan Douglas Merritt, ca. 1870*

Merritt art gallery. *Courtesy the collection of Mrs. Alan Douglas Merritt, ca. 1870.*

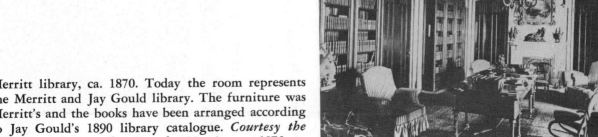

Merritt library, ca. 1870. Today the room represents the Merritt and Jay Gould library. The furniture was Merritt's and the books have been arranged according to Jay Gould's 1890 library catalogue. *Courtesy the collection of Mrs. Alan Douglas Merritt, ca. 1870.*

Paulding's Gothic drawing room as modernized by Merritt. *Courtesy the collection of Mrs. Alan Douglas Merritt, ca. 1870.*

Dining room, showing original furniture designed by architect Davis. *Courtesy National Trust for Historic Preservation, Sleepy Hollow Studio, 1964.*

Lyndhurst and grounds, showing the greenhouse, laundry-guest house at the left, and north gatehouse at the top. *Courtesy Dolega Studios, ca. 1950.*

Central portion of the Merritt greenhouse. *Courtesy the collection of Mrs. Alan Douglas Merritt, ca. 1870.*

] 10 [

PRATT'S CASTLE

OVERLOOKING THE JAMES RIVER IN RICHMOND, Virginia, once stood a lofty, turreted structure known as Pratt's Castle. Since its construction in 1853–54, this structure was also referred to as Pratt's Place, Pratt's Folly, and Pratt's Cottage. This interesting castellated structure built on Gamble's Hill, was the work of William Abbott Pratt, who was born in Sutton, England, on March 7, 1818.

In the year 1832, William Abbott Pratt senior, and his wife, Elizabeth Stevens Pratt, immigrated with their young son to the United States, where they settled for a short time in Washington, afterward moving to the city of Alexandria. Young William Pratt soon began his studies in architecture and civil engineering, rapidly excelling in these professions to become division engineer in charge of the Chesapeake and Ohio Canal, at the early age of eighteen.

He married Evelina Ginevan, of Hampshire County, Virginia (now West Virginia), on June 17, 1838, and later, in 1845, he took his family to settle in Richmond, Virginia. Among his many interests, the extremely talented Pratt made studies of the intriguing art of Daguerre, an early method of photography. In 1846 he was soon to establish and become proprietor of the first "Skylight Daguerreon Gallery at the Sign of the Gothic Window," on Main Street in Richmond. During this early venture at his gallery, which was a forerunner of today's photographic studios, he took some thirty-five thousand portraits, and his inventiveness led him to conceive

the idea of taking four pitcures on a single photographic plate.

The unique structure in Virginia that was to become Pratt's castle residence, was for many years the subject of much comment and speculation. Seen at a distance the castle was seemingly constructed entirely of grey stone, but a closer inspection revealed that, due to clever adaption of architectural building materials, this was not the case. With the exception of the ground floor, which is built of stone quarried from the James River, the upper walls and turrets were constructed of wood with a covering of sheet metal of various sizes painted to simulate a solid stonework appearance. Other stone used on the project was in the construction of a high, battlemented wall that completely surrounded the building. This wall was erected years after the castle had been built, an undertaking that was similarly done with some of the ancient castles in Europe after their construction.

Passing through the iron wall gate, which was flanked by two battlemented wall columns, two flights of steps led to the upper entrance door. The main circular tower had windows on each floor and an additional smaller, circular, battlemented tower rising from its roof. Two additional high towers flanked another lower entrance with its heavy door, and rose above the battlemented roof structure. The wall to the right of the circular tower, near the base of the stairs leading to the upper entrance, was faced with four windows, each of which was canopied in an interesting sheet-metal design. The balcony extending across the lower two windows of this wall, and whose ends met both the main circular tower and another tower, appeared to have been added at a later date since it was not seen in the early engraving or in the photograph of 1865. This upper main entrance also underwent some revisions in its architecture so that the enclosed glass wall and entrance door were fronted by a porch and overhanging battlemented roof extension not previously shown on the original design. On the upper roof connecting the towers and chimneys was a low, battlemented wall enclosing the entire roof area with access stairs from the main circular tower to the roof. The view from this roof over the James River has been described as one unequalled from any other place in Richmond at the time.

Many interesting odd-shaped rooms of various sizes and numerous small and unique staircases composed the interior of this structure, with the notable feature that no single room had the same ceiling height. In addition to the small tower rooms there was a living room, dining room, kitchen, reception hall, sleeping chambers, and various storage rooms. Other interesting rooms included the Park Room, containing the lowest ceiling and so named because of its location facing the park, and the Halfway Room located midway between the first and second floors. A legend regarding these rooms indicates that Edgar Allan Poe once used the Park Room to compose some of his stories, and the Halfway Room as his sleeping quarters.

Only a few years before this structure was razed, a dungeon was discovered while a furnace was being installed. This mysterious chamber was reached by a secret spiral staircase near the reception room that also gave access to the kitchen. The dungeon was a small, square, windowless room with four air vent holes and a stone floor. The actual use of this chamber remains a mystery although it is believed that it may have been used to store guns and ammunition during the American Civil War. During these war years Pratt was in sympathy with the Confederacy and is believed to have made several trips to England in 1862 to secure munitions for their cause.

Originally a dining room, the basement center room contained a large fireplace that was in constant use for each entire day. The main dining room in use had no windows but obtained its daylight from other surrounding rooms. At one time this dining room, and adjoining living room, contained two matched glass chandeliers brought about half a century earlier from the Crystal Palace in London. These beautifully designed chandeliers supplied gas through their hollow glass tubing without the use of metal pipes.

Folding paneled doors connected the dining room with the living room, which once contained several objects and furniture of historical significance. The living room ceiling was square-patterned in inset wood panels with an octagonal, wood-design centerpiece from which hung one of the glass chandeliers. On either side of geometrically patterned stained-glass windows were narrow, glass-paneled doors, each leading to the smaller turrets located on that side of the building.

Near the living room was a most unusual spiral staircase that led to the main tower. Believed to have been one of the first circular staircases in America, the steps were constructed of wrought iron with similarly patterned risers. The uniquely designed rail was also of wrought iron but with a hand rest of rope fastened to a supporting iron frame.

In contrast to several rectangular glass-paneled doorways there were interior doorways of Gothic design paneled with glass. Gothic-designed windows were also found in contrast to rectangular windows of various exterior walls including the main tower.

There were other features often commented on in connection with this castle structure, such as a secret passage to the river that was closed in when Fourth Street, adjoining the castle, was constructed through to Gamble's Hill.

As representative of the Society of Alumni of the University of Virginia, Pratt undertook a plan in 1855 of procuring a copy of Paul Balze's painting of Raphael's School of Athens, on their behalf. Pratt acted as agent of the University, giving it custody of the painting for three years during which time proceeds from exhibits would defray the cost. The picture was exhibited in the United States and also in England in 1856. Several lectures in philosophy and art were given by Pratt during the exhibits, and by February of 1857 Balze's painting was formally presented to the University of Virginia. In 1858 the University employed Pratt as superintendent of grounds and buildings of the University after his first managing the architectural arrangements for a new public hall that was also to contain the Balze painting.

William A. Pratt continued in this capacity with the University until January, 1862, when he was called upon to make several trips to Europe on behalf of the Confederate States. In 1863, after about one year's absence, he continued his activities and plans at the University of Virginia until the close of the war.

Pratt had three sons. The eldest, Captain G. Julian Pratt, had been a student at the University of Virginia, where he enlisted in a company called "Sons of Liberty," formed from the student body. Under this organization he took part in the campaign at Harper's Ferry, remaining under this enlistment until it was disbanded by Governor Wise of Virginia. Reenlisting, he served through the Civil War under General Jubal A. Early. Pratt's two other sons were Captain William A. Pratt, a distinguished civil engineer connected with the Baltimore and Ohio Railroad, and Dr. Charles E. Pratt, who lived in Wheeling, West Virginia.

In 1865 Pratt sold his castle residence and took living quarters at Charlottesville, and later moved to Staunton, in 1867. He practiced in the field of architecture in Staunton for several years, retiring for a short time at his Walnut Grove farm near Waynesboro, where on January 18, 1879, he passed away.

Pratt's Castle has passed to other owners since Pratt first sold it. The castle was a familiar landmark in Richmond for many years. On December 9, 1945, the castle was seriously damaged by fire but was restored only to be damaged again by fire in February, 1951. The castle was altered somewhat by successive owners and after each of the two fires.

In the late fall of 1957 a city block in Richmond that included Pratt's Castle was to be razed to make way for the headquarters of a paper-manufacturing company. Thus ended another structure unique in its style of architecture with its rambling corridors, unusual stairways and battlements, tower and walls. Today it remains only as a vivid memory with legends and stories intermingled with its relatively short history.

The first known picture of Pratt's Castle taken from an engraving on a coupon distributed by Pratt between 1853 and 1858. *Courtesy the Valentine Museum, Richmond, Virginia.*

Pratt's Castle from a drawing by T. H. Wilkinson. *Courtesy Dementi Studio, Richmond, Virginia.*

This photo of Pratt's Castle shows the battlemented brick wall with entrance. Note the sheet metal canopies over the windows. The stair on the roof gave access to the main tower. *Courtesy Dementi Studio, Richmond, Virginia, 1957.*

At a distance, Pratt's Castle appears to be of stone construction. Stairs lead to the main entrance. *Courtesy
Dementi Studio, Richmond, Virginia, 1957.*

Pratt's Castle on Gable Hill, Richmond, Virginia, 1865.
Courtesy Brady Photo. Reproduced from the collections of the Library of Congress.

Believed to be one of the first spiral staircases in America. Note the iron steps and rope of the hand-railing. *Courtesy Dementi Studio, Richmond, Virginia.*

This recessed arched door leads to the entry way.
Courtesy Dementi Studio, Richmond, Virginia.

This entry shows walls curving inward to the ceiling.
The entry door is very plain as compared to the arched
interior doorway. *Courtesy Dementi Studio, Richmond,
Virginia.*

The stained-glass window is seen centered between two small towers. One of the tower doors is sealed. Note the glass chandelier. *Courtesy Dementi Studio, Richmond, Virginia.*

Pratt's Castle, 1900–1906. The stained-glass window is seen above the arched door and between the two smaller towers. The balcony is not shown as constructed in the 1865 photograph. *Courtesy the Valentine Museum, Richmond, Virginia.*

] 11 [

OLD STATE CAPITOL

THE OLD STATE CAPITOL LOCATED IN BATON Rouge, Louisiana was first constructed during the period of 1847 to 1850. The state of Louisiana had shifted its seat of government several times, and in 1846, after a long and difficult struggle, the General Assembly fixed the location of the state capitol in Baton Rouge. Representatives were appointed to choose a site, appoint an architect, and participate in the supervision for the erection of a state capitol building.

The city of Baton Rouge had donated 120,000 square feet of property upon which the structure was erected overlooking the great Mississippi River. The man chosen for the task of constructing the new statehouse was James Harrison Dakin, a fine architect and builder of his day, who had been a colonel in the military during the Mexican-American War. Dakin faithfully recorded the interesting events concerning the building of this structure in his red, leather diary. He related his adaptation of a style of architecture that would give the building a distinctive and classic character suitable for its purpose. In his design, Dakin used castellated Gothic as being an appropriate architectural style in its commanding character.

Plans called for a structure 137 by 130 feet containing forty-two rooms or apartments. In early November of 1847 the cornerstone was laid with great pomp and appropriate ceremonies witnessed by a large attendance of the townspeople and others from surrounding areas.

Though Dakin kept close records of expenditures, as close to one half cent in some instances, the construction of the statehouse posed many difficulties, delays, and trying experiences for him. The keen eye of the architect inspected the building materials closely to assure their quality. On one occasion tempers flared when Dakin discovered that a substandard brick was being furnished. A partner of the company supplying the bricks thought he could make some extra money at the expense of the taxpayers by substituting the poor grade of brick, but this was soon corrected by the architect in an exchange of fisticuffs. This contest of blows did little damage to either of the two men but did result in an improvement in the quality of forthcoming shipments of bricks. The castellated statehouse is essentially a brick structure faced with a covering of cement. Cast iron was used for the window frames and other ornamentations.

By midsummer of 1849, the building was completed with work on the large interior chambers and halls well underway. Dedication of the new state capitol building was set for December 1 of that year, and the citizens of Baton Rouge had contributed several thousands of dollars to assure suitable ceremonies and festivities planned for the great occasion. Unfortunately, a disastrous fire occurred only about a week prior to the official opening of the building. Nearly a fifth of the city was consumed in flames, but the statehouse was spared since the devastated area was not near the new biulding. At the suggestion of Isaac Johnson, governor of the state at that time, the funds that were to be used for the dedication were made available to aid the victims of the fire. The dedication did take place on December 1 but without the originally planned festivities.

Alterations and additions have been made on the building over the years and it is a story higher than the original structure. There are two main entrances, each located directly opposite the other with broad, high doorways. These entranceways are set within white-marble-exterior wall facades that join turreted towers four stories high, projecting several feet above the marble wall facades. At one main entrance the two towers are octagonal in design, while the opposite main entrance towers are square. All four towers contain windows of similar design at each of the four levels. Beautiful great Gothic windows of intricate design are centrally located in these marble facades extending from the second floor to a height of approximately one and a half stories. Other Gothic windows are found in the structure where the House and Senate chambers were located.

In addition to the towers, battlements enclose the entire roof perimeter at its various levels. A patterned cornice surrounds the turrets and principal central building portion below the battlements, with exterior doors and windows covered with moldings of various shapes. Immediately behind the towers, at both ends of the building, are two-story-high building sections that adjoin the four-story-high main central portion of the structure. Above the other building levels is a large, square, centrally located top level on the main portion of the statehouse. This section is entirely enclosed in glass by a series of narrow Gothic windows on each side. The exterior wall perimeter above these windows once had battlements that were later removed with alterations to the building.

Surrounding the capitol building and its beautiful grounds was an ornate cast-iron fence made by a foundry in the city. It was an attractive and well-designed enclosure with cast panels, recurring symbols of the fleur-de-lis, and gate posts mounted by castings of imposing eagles fashioned with outspread wings.

In late January of 1850, the first meeting of the Legislature took place in the new capitol building.

James Dakin died on May 10, 1852, only three months after he considered his work completed on the new building. He had officially conveyed the building over to the state in February of that year. A gas lighting plant was installed during midyear of 1857, providing modern lighting within the building.

With the coming of the Civil War, Baton Rouge was occupied by Union forces in 1862, and the capitol building was imprudently used as a barracks with troops quartered there a few days before Christmas. On the 28 of December a minor fire broke out in the biulding while the troops were preparing supper, but efforts of the firemen and some federal soldiers managed to subdue the flames. In the early hours of the following morning another fire was discovered that had already gained considerable progress. The efforts of civilians and troops to arrest the rapidly spreading flames were hopeless. The interior of the entire structure, with its magnificent state library, was completely consumed in the flames, leaving only the shell of the firm walls standing.

Because of the war, the building was not immediately reconstructed. The gates being left open at the time caused the beautifully landscaped grounds with their rare trees and shrubs to be destroyed by cattle, horses, and senseless human vandalism. But this situation was corrected by order of the provost guard. Gardeners were employed to restore the grounds, which gradually regained their former splendor.

After having used other buildings in New Orleans for quarters, the capitol was voted to return to Baton Rouge after the 1878 election, and in the early 1880s appropriations for funds were made for the reconstruction of the Baton Rouge state capitol building. Architect William A. Freret was appointed to reconstruct the building, and in doing so he added a new story to the building's central portion. Leading from the central hall of the building, a gracefully curved iron staircase, designed by the architect, was installed leading to the second floor. Adjacent to the inner curve of this staircase is a single iron column leading up to a multipaneled, colored-glass dome. This large dome is supported by numerous curved, structural members branching out in a circular, curving pattern from the upper portion of the central column.

Small, elaborate, cast-iron turrets were added on top of the towers but were unpopular during their existence and removed during renovations to the building in 1937. Several of the chambers contained marble mantels and ornate chandeliers of unique design, which added to the stateliness of the rooms. By March 1, 1882, renovations of the capitol building were completed, with the government's administration branch fully settled in the State House. In early 1894 the building was wired for the newly installed electric lighting fixtures.

The venerable Old State Capitol, with its lovely terraced gardens and stately atmosphere within its walls, continued to function in its capacity until 1932. Up to this time the growth of the state continued to expand, and gradually the Old State Capitol became inadequate quarters. In May, 1932, government administration offices officially abandoned the Old State Capitol, taking quarters in a new modern, thirty-four-story structure in another part of the city, leaving the old building for use by emergency federal agencies.

The Old State Capitol soon gathered dust and gave way to deterioration and seekers of souvenirs. Through the years the beautiful marble mantels received a coating of black paint and the building was marred further by vandals who broke numerous panes of imported stained glass in the rotunda.

During the period of 1937 to 1938 a program to renovate the Old State Capitol began that greatly enhanced the appearance of the structure and its grounds as it had been when first built. In addition to interior repairs, steam heating was installed, the old elevator was put into proper working order, and the marble mantels were restored to their original natural finish, as were the colored lights and glass of the rotunda. The roof received new copper and the exterior walls were coated in stone grey with aluminum silver on the window trims with ledges in black. The grounds were landscaped with lawns, evergreens, and magnolia trees, in addition to varieties of flowering shrubs.

The building became headquarters of various federal offices and other agencies by an act of the Legislature in 1938. Rich in an atmosphere of a historic past, the Old State Capitol thus restored was indeed a grand, castellated structure of appealing architectural beauty. Additional minor repairs were made to the building in 1947, and in 1950 restoration of the old, cast-iron fence was completed. To preserve the building as a World War II war memorial, the Old State Capitol Memorial Commission was created by the Legislature in 1948.

Since the major renovations in 1937 another drive to improve the Old State Capitol was authorized by the Legislature in 1955. Such improvements included the installation of fire doors and an automatic fire sprinkler system. Exhibit rooms were introduced, as were new colors to interior rooms and the rotunda. Old lighting fixtures were stored until funds could be made available to properly restore them. Several rooms in the basement were to be converted into a war museum for public viewing, and an air conditioning system was installed for the visitors' comfort. The exterior of the building was repainted, as was the iron fence surrounding the grounds.

In order to stress the historic value of the Old State Capitol and to restore it to the beauty of its former days in the late nineteenth century, a new program of restoration was begun in 1968. The elevator and the electric lighting would be retained, but the fixtures used would be those designed of the early period. The central heating system would utilize the old fireplaces with air ducts connected to them, thus eliminating units that were visible in several of the rooms. The rooms would also be returned to their former dimensions with the elimination of partitions that once provided office cubicles in previous renovations. The stored chandeliers and lights would again hang from the ceilings with lamps placed on the rotunda's spiral staircase as in former days. Other improvements and restorations include the return of original doors and their former tinted window panes, in addition to exposing previously covered grillwork, and removing of partitions from behind lacy woodwork that obscured their relief.

Though the Old State Capitol has been renovated many times since its erection began in 1847, its castellated, Gothic architecture conceived by James Dakin still presents a noble structure engrossed in the history of the Old South. As with riverboats that once graced the Mississippi, the tranquil Southern life of the past is recalled in the picturesque Old State Capitol where Louisiana's history was made by men who once passed through its echoing halls.

An early photograph of the Old State Capitol after
the metal turrets were erected. A portion of the iron
fence surrounding the grounds is shown. *Courtesy the
collections of the Library of Congress.*

Old State Capitol, showing several of the battlemented
turrets before they were removed. The battlements of
the upper central portion of the building above the
series of Gothic windows are also shown. These battlements and the small turrets were removed during later
renovations. *Courtesy Louisiana State Library.*

Facade of the Old State Capitol, showing marble entry and large Gothic window. This portion between the two towers was made entirely of marble. At the opposite end of the building the facade is very similar except towers are of square design. *Courtesy Louisiana State Library.*

Old State Capitol, showing absence of small turrets and battlements of the upper central portion. The series of Gothic windows in this upper portion is clearly evident. *Courtesy Louisiana State Library.*

The upper portion of the column changes in design as it branches out its supporting members to the beautiful multipaneled, colored-glass ceiling. *Courtesy Louisiana State Library.*

The curved staircase. The octagonal shaft within the curve leads up to the glass-domed ceiling. *Courtesy Louisiana State Library.*

] 12 [

VANDERPOEL CASTLE

AMBROSE ELY VANDERPOEL WAS THE LAST OF A Dutch family that began farming in Summit, New Jersey, in the early 1700s. His parents, George and Maria Vanderpoel, also had two daughters, Julia Louise and Catherine Ann, both of whom died in early childhood. Ambrose, their third child, was frail, like his mother, but alert and intelligent as his cultured parents. Born in 1875, Ambrose never attended the public schools but received his education from tutors until he obtained a degree in law. He opened a law office in Madison but fought only a single case. It is believed that because of their great wealth, his mother felt that Ambrose should give up his law practice to more needy lawyers. Ambrose took his mother's advice, turning to helping in the management of the Vanderpoel estate and writing several books, one of which was a history of Chatham, New Jersey.

Local history records the first Vanderpoel about 1770. Being a tanner and currier, he also acquired much farmland bordering the Passaic River. It is said that his daughter was the cause of much local gossip when romance developed between her and a relative of the Marquis de Lafayette, Count Joseph Louis d'Anterroches. They were married in Madison and lived happily with their eventual brood of ten children.

Earlier, in 1872, Ambrose's grandfather had demolished their old colonial farmhouse to improve the property with the building of a commodious wood-framed mansion. This structure was to be used as a summer house for the family who lived in New York, but the project was abandoned before being completed, due to the death of his wife. Grandfather Vanderpoel gave the property to his son George and his wife Maria, who continued the work on the mansion, completing it in 1872. The grandfather took a great interest in the mansion, sending furniture, statuary, and other objects for the new summer house.

On December 31, 1882, while the Vanderpoels were at their winter house in New York, a fire of undetermined origin broke out at the summer mansion. The fire was discovered that Sunday morning by the caretaker, who lived with his son in the mansion's basement apartments. The caretaker's son was sent in haste to the Presbyterian Church in Chatham to summon help. All the men of the gathered congregation quickly responded but arrived too late to save the wooden structure that was blazing beyond control. The men did manage to save most of the fine furniture and some chandeliers from the portion of the house that was not yet consumed by the spreading fire.

In 1884 George and Maria Vanderpoel spent two summers with the neighbor who had notified them of the fire, during the time their new home was being constructed at the site of the destroyed mansion. The addition of stone and brick enhanced the new, castellated structure, which contained about twenty-five rooms on four floors with several battlemented towers of various shapes and elevations. The Vanderpoel Castle, as it became known, was completed in 1885, but the thought of the previous disaster still lingered with the family. Grandfather Vanderpoel had made an extensive tour of Europe during which time he wrote to George and Maria to guard against burglars. Maria was a thoughtful and generous person, but naturally frail and delicate. The warnings of grandfather's letter, and perhaps past experience, resulted in the hiring of two guards who patrolled the castle estate on foot seven days a week. Each guard worked twelve hours, one on days, the other at nights, both punching five time clocks during their tour of duty, consisting of guarding against fires and prowlers.

The ornate, iron entrance gates of the main entry driveway were set in the thick, stone wall that ran at varying heights along the front of the property. White globe lamps flanked these gates with similar globe pole lamps spaced along the drive that led to a circular drive at the main castle entry. The entrance portico was flanked by parapeted octagonal towers that rose to the height of the roof. To the right of this entrance was the great, rectangular main tower, rising two stories above the roof and other corner towers. This battlemented central tower contained one room on each of its four floors above the ground and first floors. These two lower floors below the central tower were partitioned as part of these lower floor rooms, not having a tower outline as the rooms above. The lower corner towers were occupied by roomy alcoves on each of the three floors. The roof perimeter joining the lower corner towers was parapeted with access to this flat roof and the high central tower roof, each offering excellent views. One of the corner towers had circular, petite turrets rising above the roof with rectangular and shallow-arched windows on the towers and the main building walls. A broad, white, ornate trim encircled the upper exterior walls just below the battlements with white, narrow trim bordering the windows of the main building and its towers.

Other exterior portions of the castle had pitched roofs with dormer windows projecting out. The contrast of this portion of the castle was evident here but blending in a pleasing manner peculiar to the structure's architecture.

The interior rooms were spacious, with some carved fireplaces showing excellent craftsmanship in the intricate, patterned designs, as in the dining and drawing rooms. The main heating system of the rooms used the facilities of radiators of various dimensions that were painted to blend with the particular room interior. Chandeliers of varying ornate designs hung from the ceilings of some rooms, each suited to the interior docoration and purpose of the rooms.

Exterior, two-story, wood-frame buildings, barn, and stables were also on the property, which included a large duck pond and extensive gardens. Since Ambrose never married, he was left alone after his mother died at age seventy-seven, when Ambrose was in his forties, and his father passed away three years later.

Ambrose Vanderpoel spent much of his time working on the castle estate, caring for the gardens, and working the farm machinery. Mondays were set aside for business in New York. On Sundays he attended the Presbyterian Church in Chatham, announcing the services by ringing the bell he had presented to the church. Ambrose lived at the castle until 1940, when he died of pneumonia at the age of sixty-five. He left the castle and the greater bulk of his assets to the Masonic Home and Charity Foundation at Burlington, with large sums of money willed to other home institutions.

In 1942 the Masons sold the castle and part of the property to the Zahodiakin Engineering Corporation, which erected a small building for its business where the stables had stood. Victor F. Zahodiakin and his family occupied the Vanderpoel Castle as a one-family residence except for help and maids' quarters. When Mrs. Tania Zahodiakin was widowed, she and her children continued to live at the castle that they had furnished and cherished as their home.

In 1968 the New Jersey Highway Department made plans for a freeway that required the demolition of the Vanderpoel Castle. All efforts by the owner to save the building were unsuccessful, and the castle became the property of the Highway Department and was scheduled to be razed.

The Vanderpoel Castle will long be remembered as one of the finest structures of its kind, with lofty, battlemented towers silhouetted against an evening sky. Its role as a castellated dwelling was cherished not only by the Zahodiakin family, but also by the generations of people who looked upon the castle in Union County as a familiar landmark and reminder of days gone by.

Vanderpoel Castle, showing a portion of the main central tower and corner turreted towers. *Courtesy the Newark News.*

Vanderpoel Castle showing contrasting architecture. Note the enclosed screen porch. *Courtesy Chatham Historical Society.*

The circular drive to the main entry of the castle. The battlemented towers and roof perimeter are clearly shown with white contrasting trim. *Courtesy Chatham Historical Society.*

Vanderpoel Castle as it existed before the fire. A portion of this architecture including the brick octagonal tower still remains. *Courtesy the Chatham Historical Society.*

Entrance to the Vanderpoel estate showing one of the guards at his post. The guards maintained a twenty-four-hour watch over the castle grounds guarding against fires and prowlers. *Courtesy the Chatham Historical Society.*

Dining room in Vanderpoel Castle. *Courtesy the Chatham Historical Society.*

Drawing room with carved fireplace and ornate chandelier. *Courtesy Chatham Historical Society.*

] 13 [

HEARST CASTLE

THE BEGINNING OF THE HEARST CASTLE, NEAR San Simeon, California, can perhaps be said to have commenced in 1865 when William Randolph Hearst's father purchased a forty-thousand-acre landsite known as Piedra Blanca Ranch. This property, which lay adjacent to San Simeon Bay, was later expanded to 240,000 acres of mountains and valleys, and included an ocean frontage of over fifty miles.

William's father, George Hearst, made his millions in mining. His character was in great contrast to his bride to be, Phoebe Apperson, whom George met in Missouri. Her parents disapproved of her marrying the roughneck who gambled for high stakes, cursed, and chewed tobacco in an unsightly manner. Miss Apperson was a refined and cultured schoolteacher, about one half the age of the forty-one-year-old George Hearst, when they eloped.

They lived in San Francisco, where their son, William, was born in 1863. In later years young William and his mother toured Europe's cultural centers. It was here that William first came in contact with the great castles and exquisite works of art that fascinated him and drew his attention throughout his lifetime.

In those days, after his father had acquired the San Simeon Bay property, William Hearst enjoyed life at the ranch where in the late 1870s his father held informal parties at an elevated campsite. It was a wonderful place where one could fish for trout in the streams and hunt the varieties of wild game, or go riding over the miles of plains and valleys of the ranch. Young William spent many carefree days and nights at this campsite, which offered a splendid panoramic view of the mountains and the sea. This "enchanted hill" was a place of strong sentimental attachment for William that was to remain with him in later life.

After having attended Harvard University where, in addition to his studies, he had a few romances, drank beer, and had himself expelled by presenting packaged gifts of chamber pots to his professors, he returned to California to take up a career in journalism. His father had acquired the San Francisco Examiner news paper but gave it to William, who further developed it under his critical eye and passion for dramatic journalism.

When George Hearst died in 1891, ownership of the San Simeon Ranch was succeeded to his wife Phoebe, with the campsite hill remaining a retreat for family and guests well after the turn of the century. But camping on the hill gradually became a more luxurious experience for guests a few years later. A complete tent village awaited them, which included a dining hall, social hall, and sleeping quarters, set up for a few weeks each summer.

William Hearst and his wife, Millicent Willson Hearst, were married in 1903. They maintained residences in New York City and Long Island where they lived with their five children.

It was during these years that the vigorous William Hearst expanded his newspaper chain, which, together with other activities, occupied much of his time, thus making only brief stays at the hilltop campsite possible. After his mother's death in 1919, the property was passed to William, whose subsequent visits to the California ranch made it his headquarters. Plans for the campsite were soon developed to transform it into a permanent home in the form of a large rambling castle. The planning called for quarters for guests, then the main castle structure where Hearst was to take up residence. These structures were also to provide appropriate accommodations for the owner's vast and growing collection of antiques and art objects.

In the fall of 1919 work commenced on the first of a group of three "cottages" as guest quarters. These three buildings were named according to their views. Casa Del Mar is exposed to the sea view of the Pacific Ocean; La Casa Del Monte faces the Santa Lucia Mountains; and La Casa Del Sol views the setting sun. These Spanish renaissance-style buildings, with their red, tile roofs, contain up to eighteen rooms in La Casa Del Mar, the first of the three permanent structures to rise on the former camp ground. These buildings were located on terrain so as to be one story high in front and three stories high on their outer side. This afforded the use of balconies and loggias on the outward face of the building thus providing excellent views of the countryside.

The west-facing loggia of La Casa Del Mar has a number of original ancient, stone columns of Egyptian porphyry, said to have come from Jerusalem. Hearst lived in this lovely dwelling while the main building was being constructed. Many beautiful objects adorn and are built into these three structures whose courtyards are ornamented with iron grillwork and antique statues. The elaborately designed bed of Cardinal Richelieu occupies a room in La Casa Del Monte. Other treasures throughout these buildings include ancient marble mantels, carved ceilings, doorways, chests, and several tapestries and rugs of intriguing design. Interior rooms have walls adorned with friezes representing nymphs, cherubs, and other such subjects.

Before work had been finished on the third "cottage," construction had begun on the main castle building, La Casa Grande, the great house. Hearst frequently consulted with his architect, Miss Julia Morgan, a graduate of the Beaux Arts in Paris. She

succeeded admirably in this great undertaking, which posed many difficulties of building and rebuilding to suit Hearst's constant change in plans, additions, and altering in designs to accommodate newly acquired treasures.

The main building was begun in 1922 with plans calling for over one hundred rooms, which included thirty-eight bedrooms, fourteen sitting rooms, thirty-one bathrooms, two large libraries, assembly hall, refectory, billiard room, movie theater, and kitchens. This large structure was to be in a setting of 123 acres of gardens and terraces in addition to elaborate outdoor and indoor pools. The main facade is flanked by a pair of towering Spanish Renaissance campaniles composed of marble lacework tower windows, sculptured stone balustrades, and copper domes, housing bronze carillons from Belgium. After passing through the elaborately designed and impressive entranceway, one finds the spacious chamber of the vestibule to contain a mosaic flooring whose central portion, dating from the first century A.D., was brought from Pompeii and installed by Italian artisans.

The large, rectangular chamber of the assembly hall is perhaps one of the most impressive in the castle, with walls two stories high and enclosing a space one hundred by forty-two feet. The intricately carved, coffered ceiling, some twenty-two feet above the floor, was brought from Italy and installed without alterations. Centered at both end walls are sets of marble medallions carved in Denmark, each weighing one ton. A great, carved, stone fireplace mantel, dating from the sixteenth century, is located on one of the side walls. Seventeenth-century Flemish tapestries hang over ancient, high-backed and elaborately carved wood choir stalls that once occupied an old Italian monastery. Other features of this interesting room are gilded doorway frames, and behind one of the wall panels is an elevator that once carried Hearst from his private quarters above into the assembly room, where he greeted his guests who gathered there each evening before passing into the refectory for dinner. Numerous antiques, such as tables, benches, chairs, and chests, fill the room, blending with its rich setting.

The refectory is said to be Hearst's favorite room. Perhaps the most notable feature in this large dining hall is its beautiful four-hundred-year-old dark wood ceiling brought from an Italian monastery. The ceiling is divided into a series of panels each of which contains a life-size figure of a saint, carved in high relief. At one end of the refectory is a great, Gothic mantel from an old, French chateau, and at the opposite end of the room is an arched musicians' gallery of Gothic design. Detailed tapestries depicting the prophet Daniel hang on the lower side walls, while the upper portions contain numerous Sienese banners mounted on poles. Many choice furnishings, such as the refectory's monastic dining tables, leather-backed chairs, and several detailed silver pieces, add to the medieval setting of this beautiful room.

Another spacious chamber is the comfortably furnished morning room, lavish in its style and antiques. This room, with its many outstanding fifteenth-century objects, was once a favorite gathering place of the castle's prominent guests. A large, Gothic mantel, of French origin, and elaborate in design, stands at one end of the room whose Spanish moresque ceiling dates from the fifteenth century.

Many excellent tapestries hang in the elegant game room, where recreation is found in the form of billiards and pool. Another form of entertainment is the movie theater, which could accommodate fifty guests in the elaborate loge seats with space for an additional fifty if necessary. Antique, red brocade paneling lines the walls, which are lighted at intervals by carved figures holding torches. The passageway leading to this theater contains a console with a keyboard used in sounding the carillon bells of the great towers.

Another impressive and spacious room is the second-floor library located above the assembly hall. This large chamber, nearly one hundred feet long, contains a beautifully designed wooden ceiling acquired from a sixteenth century Italian palace. The cabinets that line the walls contain over five thousand handsomely bound volumes, many of which are rare editions. Much exquisite furniture of the Louis XVI period is found here, in addition to a valuable collection of urns, vases, and Egyptian pottery that rests on shelves along with many other antique objects.

The Gothic study, on the third floor, is one of the most unusual and beautifully designed rooms to be found in the castle. The main contribution to the style of this room is the series of Spanish Gothic arches, each of which is elaborately detailed with carved, painted figures and scenes. The lower portions of the side walls spanning the arches are lined with iron-grilled bookcases containing hundreds of books. Set in above the bookcases are rare, stained-glass panes set in clerestory windows.

In one of the twin towers, on the top, fourth floor, is the group of rooms called the Celestial Suite, containing two bedrooms and a connecting sitting room. Excellent views of the ocean, mountains, and valleys are obtained from the windows of this tower apartment.

The Doge's Room, with its beautiful, ornate ceiling and fireplace mantel, contains numerous art objects and antique furnishings of intricate design and detail. The numerous rooms throughout La Casa Grande contain a seemingly endless array of antiques, art objects, tapestries, and furnishings spanning a vast period of time, as does much of the Old-World architecture built into and around the building.

One of the most remarkable creations of the estate are the swimming pools, one indoors and a second outdoors. The indoor Roman pool, located to the rear of La Casa Grande, was the last major structure to be completed on the hill. Its size is such that two tennis courts were laid out on its roof. With an estimated cost of one million dollars, and nearly four years of labor, crews of Italian artisans were brought in to lay the many thousands of tiny, brilliantly colored Venetian tiles, a delicate work admirably achieved by those master craftsmen. The many-colored tiles were laid in various patterns not only on the pool but also on the entire structures, floors, and walls. Exclusive of the more shallow arm of the children's pool that extends to one side, the main pool measures eighty by forty feet with a total capacity of two hundred thousand gallons of water.

The beautiful, oval-shaped, outdoor Neptune pool is constructed entirely of marble. Slabs of white marble are laid in pattern on the pool's floor, whose longest length measured 104 feet. Being the favorite of the guests, its three hundred forty-five thousand gallons of water were kept heated at a constant seventy degrees when Hearst occupied the estate. Marble colonnades circle the ends of this pool and on one side in a splendid setting is a well-proportioned Grecian-Roman temple facade. In the pediment of this temple is a sculptured figure of Neptune, flanked by two sea nymphs riding on dolphins. It is from this sculptured group that the pool derives its name. Many beautiful sculptured figures surround the pool with stairways leading to terraced gardens.

Some two thousand acres of hillside and canyon grounds were set aside to accommodate the variety of animals that were to freely roam this area. An eight-foot-high wire fence, ten miles in length, was installed to enclose the compound. Animals were of great interest to Hearst, who collected nearly a hundred species of both domestic and jungle animals. Located a short distance downhill of the castle were the quarters of many caged birds and wild beasts whose feeding time provided an exciting diversion for the castle's guests. A few of the animals that roamed the grounds consisted of elk, kangaroos, camels, spotted deer, and giraffes. Of the caged animals and birds were several leopards, cheetahs, a gorilla, wildcats, eagles, cockatoos, and several other species of wild animals.

Many of the animals were presented to various cities on the West Coast after the zoo was abandoned in the late 1930s. But several animals remained on the grounds, adapting to the environment and increasing in number. Present-day visitors may find zebras, elk, and other such animals peacefully grazing on the surrounding hillside.

Like many other things pertaining to the "enchanted hill," the landscaping of the grounds was also done on a grand scale. Acres of trees, shrubs, and flower beds were planted in earth brought up from the meadows to add to the scarcity of soil on the hilltop. Entire lots of tall cypress trees were crated and transferred to the site, as were numerous other trees that were transplanted to suit the planned landscaping. Within the immediate area of the castle a great collection of carved figures, such as the Egyptian cat goddess, and ancient Roman sarcophagus, were placed about the many terraces and detailed, marble stairways.

During the development of the San Simeon castle, Hearst's constant companion was Miss Marion Davies, a showgirl from Brooklyn and daughter of a politician. Hearst was past fifty when reportedly he first saw the twenty-one-year-old Miss Davies in the 1917 Ziegfeld Follies. Their romance caused much gossip, to say the least, as she accompanied him on numerous tours of Europe while he collected the many treasures for the castle. Many of the guests at the castle were world-famous personalities such as Sir

Winston Churchill and George Bernard Shaw, and numerous renowned show people such as Carole Lombard, Dick Powell, Charlie Chaplin, Errol Flynn, and Buster Keaton, to mention just a very few.

At the outbreak of the Second World War, more than half of the total land area of the ranch, amounting to 140,000 acres, was sold to the United States government as a training ground for troops, and is now known as the Hunter Liggett Military Reservation. In 1946 the eighty-four-year-old Hearst suffered a heart attack and was advised by his physicians to move to a place less isolated from the facilities of medical attention. The following few years were spent in Southern California, but his hopes of returning to San Simeon were never realized. At the age of eighty-eight Hearst grew physically weaker as the months passed, and in mid-August of 1951 the end came.

The Hearst Castle estate remained unoccupied for a long period of time, except for a group of caretakers who attended to the grounds and watched over the vast treasures, purchases of which averaged a million dollars a year for fifty years. Complete monasteries and medieval castles that had been among the purchases were carefully dismantled, packed, and shipped to the building site.

During his lifetime, Hearst expressed his wish that the estate be given to the state of California to be a cultural center for the advancement of art and culture of Californians and the public at large. Approximately a year after Hearst's death, the castle, with its contents and about 125 acres of surrounding grounds, was offered to the people of California as a gift in memorial to William Randolph Hearst and his mother, Phoebe Apperson Hearst. In 1954 the first step of the transfer was completed, and in early 1958 the title to the property was formally passed. The castle was opened to the public on June 2, 1958, and was to be known thereafter as Hearst-San Simeon State Historical Monument.

Ample evidence shows that Hearst planned to include several additional buildings to La Cuesta Encantada. Adjoining the two wings of La Casa Grande, a four-story structure was to be built that would contain a combination ballroom and banquet hall, in addition to several other chambers to house the owner's large collections. Another guest house was to be added to the existing three, and an office and utility building were also planned for construction.

Failing health postponed these projects, which were destined never to be realized. But what remains of today's celebrated "enchanted hill" is still a fabulously built structure, composed of Old-World castles, monasteries, chateaux, and other ancient architectural features together with vast treasures of the world.

Beautiful classic objects of art are found throughout the grounds of the castle. Guest house La Casa Del Mar is pictured in the background. *Courtesy the State of California Department of Parks and Recreation.*

La Casa Grande at the front entrance with twin towers rising above the entire castle. Thirty-six carillon bells hang in the towers of the castle estate, which is said to have cost twenty million dollars during its thirty years of planning and building. *Courtesy State of California Division of Beaches and Parks.*

The Neptune pool displays an interesting pattern in marble. Across from the pool is the temple with a sculpture of Neptune from which the pool derives its name. *Courtesy State of California Division of Beaches and Parks.*

One of the guest houses of Hearst Castle. *Courtesy State of California Department of Parks and Recreation.*

The indoor Roman pool took nearly four years to complete with Italian craftsmen laying the thousands of tiny tiles. *Courtesy State of California Department of Parks and Recreation.*

The main library of La Casa Grande located on the second floor. The sixteenth-century ceiling was once part of an Italian palace. Numerous handsome antiques are found throughout this large chamber with its fine book collection, many of which are first editions. *Photo by Tom Myers, courtesy State of California Department of Parks and Recreation.*

The Gothic library was often used by Hearst as part of his private suite. The arches are highly detailed in various figures covering the entire surface. *Photo by Tom Myers, courtesy State of California Department of Parks and Recreation.*

The Doge's Room features numerous art objects with its highly carved ceiling and fireplace. *Courtesy State of California Department of Parks and Recreation.*

The game room in the left wing of La Casa Grande features an antique mantel and one of the castle's best-known tapestries. *Courtesy State of California Department of Parks and Recreation.*

The Hearst Castle refectory with its four-hundred-year-old ceiling and magnificent furnishings. The group of ancient banners bear crests of noble Sienese families. *Courtesy California Historical Society, San Francisco.*

The refectory tapestries are among many that adorn the walls of the castle. The episode pictured in the tapestry shown depicts the life of the prophet Daniel. *Courtesy California Historical Society, San Francisco.*

The Egyptian cat goddess carved in black granite is many centuries old. *Courtesy State of California Department of Parks and Recreation.*

Entrance door to La Casa Del Monte featuring some
of the beautiful objects built into the architecture of
the buildings used as guest houses. *Courtesy California
Historical Society, San Francisco.*

Entrance to Hearst Castle with highly carved detail
framing the glass doors. *Courtesy California Historical
Society, San Francisco.*

The assembly hall where Hearst and guests gathered before entering the refectory. The assembly hall is the largest room in the castle, highlighting many antiques and notable architectural features, such as the carved ceiling, choir stalls, and fireplace. *Courtesy California Historical Society, San Francisco.*

The theater in La Casa Grande features beautiful carvings with seating for guests that could accommodate one hundred persons. *Courtesy California Historical Society, San Francisco.*

Aerial view of Hearst Castle showing the main building and guest dwellings. The outdoor pool is seen in the foreground. *Courtesy U. S. Army Air Forces, National Archives.*

] 14 [

CASCO CASTLE

CASCO CASTLE WAS BUILT IN FREEPORT, MAINE, in 1902–3 by Ames F. Gerald, trotting horse financier, Fairfield inventor, and promoter of twelve electric railways in Maine. He was also known in his time as the Electric Railroad King. Gerald built Casco Castle as one of several attractions along the Portland-Brunswick trolley-car line to promote travel on this system.

The castle was constructed on a high, rocky ledge as Maine's new, high-class resort hotel of Spanish medieval architecture. The structure had the refinements and comforts of the early 1900s with modern accommodations for one hundred guests. In May, 1903, construction of the four-story-high castle, with its large basement, was well on its way to completion, with plumbers and finishers completing their work on the building. The park superintendent had a large crew of men preparing the grounds for the landscape gardener who was to complete the site with flower gardens, small lakes, and other beautifying landscape features. With such elaborate architecture and landscaping, the place was soon turned into a beautiful fairyland. Quarters for a large menagerie were completed and a baseball ground was also laid out.

The castle was essentially of timber construction, rectangular in design, with battlemented towers located at the corners and an additional larger tower in the center of the building. All towers rose one story above the principal building, the majority being of square design except for one that was circular. The battlements were uniform throughout but high with narrow openings, especially in the towers. Battlements also surrounded the roof perimeter joining the higher corner towers.

The roof overhang of the second story supported a balcony surrounding the entire structure, which provided for pleasant strolling and viewing of the entire countryside. Entrance stairways at various facades led up to the loggia on the second floor, which also surrounded the castle with large, open, square sections of uniform design for viewing.

Each of the numerous windows had awnings of similar material on the third- and fourth-story windows and towers that gave an interesting effect to the entire structure. The first floor was enclosed but surrounded with high, broad-arched windows on all sides of the building. The first floor also projected out from the main building, giving it a larger floor area than the upper floors. Beautiful, intricately designed lighting fixtures, located at the exterior stairways, were matched in pairs, each set being different in design, at the main and side entrances.

From a spring several hundred feet distant from the castle a good water service was available throughouth the building. The castle's interior contained some fifty handsome bedrooms, each having private baths with facilities for both freshwater and saltwater bathing available for guests of the castle. Eleven bedrooms were also located on the roof level, which provided an unsurpassed view as far as the eye could see, commanding the ocean, bay, mountains, and coastal scenery. The splendid dining rooms and kitchen were completed and ready for public use by July 1, 1903.

Connected by a short bridge from the top of the main castle building was the hundred-foot-high, stone lookout tower built in the manner of a feudal castle tower. The stone for the three-foot-thick tower walls had been carried by oxen and horses from the roadside of South Freeport to the top of the hill overlooking Casco Bay, from which the castle derived its name.

The high, detached, stone tower was topped by a smaller projecting circular tower, with an additional small tower adjoining at one side of the main tower's base. This large, stone tower contrasted in its ruggedness to the more refined and finished towers of the principal building.

Gerald was especially interested in preserving the natural beauty of existing trees and shrubs. In one place stood a fine, huge pine tree located on the very spot where a portion of the castle piazza was to be placed. But orders were given not to remove the tree, and thus the piazza was built around it.

Since traveling was not always convenient at that time, people remained at the hotel of their choice for the duration of their vacation instead of going from place to place. Since Casco Castle had much to offer its guests, it soon became a well-known social center. To reach the castle, guests could board the trolley cars at Portland's Union Station, or ride from Yarmouth or Freeport for only five cents per person. The trolley would then stop near the castle and let the passengers off, where they could make the rest of the way on foot. On the way to the castle visitors walked across a three-hundred-foot suspension bridge located over a chasm that fronted the castle but that was some distance from it. The castle could also be reached by steamboat, and also by a gasoline packet boat that made regular trips from Portland.

Upon reaching the castle grounds the guests had several choices of entertainment, which included watching a baseball game on the ball diamond and visiting the hotel's small zoo, with its monkeys, peacocks, and wild buffalo. Those who liked to bathe could do so in a saltwater pool dammed off in the tidal stream that flowed beneath the suspension bridge. Within the castle hotel, one could enjoy a full-course shore dinner of lobster stew, steamed clams, fried clams, and boiled lobster, all for fifty cents. After dinner one could stroll through the beautiful, formal gardens or enjoy the unobscured panoramic view from the castle tower and watch the many long banners gaily swaying in the wind with their poles mounted on the battlements of the turrets. Other entertainment such as dancing, community singing, and moonlight sailing were also available. Box lunches were packed by the hotel for the guests who wished to enjoy a day's outing by traveling to a favorite picnic area on the line.

The resort was never one for the wealthy, though the castle had several successful seasons. But the automobile was beginning to appear, and as vacations and outing habits changed, the hotel's popularity gradually began to decline. Finally, with business dropping off, Casco Castle was closed. Hotel flags were removed from the towers, awnings taken down, and the windows boarded up. The castle later reopened under the management of a Massachusetts hotel man. But after a year, business again declined and the building was closed. In 1913 Ames Gerald died, and the short-lived glory of Casco Castle was soon to come to an end.

On September 9, 1914, at five o'clock in the morning, a fire started that burned the wooden structure of the main building to the ground. Several people escaped the flaming inferno with difficulty. Some were obliged to jump from their third-story rooms, while others were rescued making their way through the smoke-filled corridors.

The Freeport firemen were summoned to the scene, but since South Freeport had no water system then, and the tide of the Harraseeket River was far out, there was no effective way of combating the fire. Another nearby residence was also totally destroyed, and several others caught fire but were saved from total destruction. Only the rugged, stone tower survived the blaze, but the steps that had led to the lookout at the top of the tower were gone, with only a few of the iron brackets that held the wooden steps in place remaining.

Following the fire the Casco Castle Company sold the tower and twenty acres of the surrounding land. The property has changed hands many times since, with the tower now being privately owned.

Today this grand, stone tower still stands as a guide to the mariner, an inspiration to the artist, and a reminder of the gay life enjoyed long ago by summer visitors to Casco Castle.

Suspended footbridge leading to the castle. The castle is seen here before its completion in 1903. *Courtesy Ray B. Lydston, Freeport, Maine.*

An electric car of the Portland and Brunswick line that brought passengers to Casco Castle, seen in the background. *Courtesy Ray B. Lydston, Freeport, Maine.*

Casco Castle under construction in 1903. *Courtesy Ray B. Lydston, Freeport, Maine.*

South entrance to Casco Castle about 1903. *Courtesy
Ray B. Lydston, Freeport, Maine.*

Casco Castle during a Republican rally about 1908.
Courtesy Ray B. Lydston, Freeport, Maine.

Casco Castle after construction showing the great tower with suspended bridge to roof of main building. *Courtesy Ray B. Lydston, Freeport, Maine.*

Panoramic view of South Freeport, Maine, showing Casco Bay and the castle at the right. *Courtesy Ray B. Lydston, Freeport, Maine.*

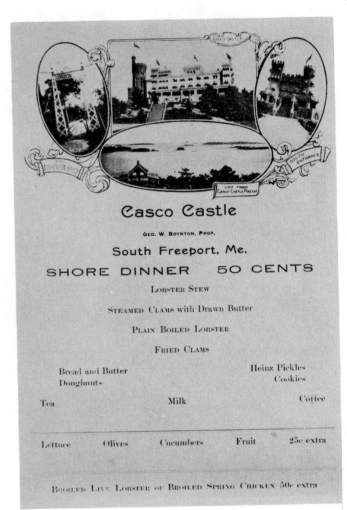

A menu of Casco Castle featuring their famous shore dinners. *Courtesy Ray B. Lydston, Freeport, Maine.*

Casco Castle as it existed before the great fire. *Courtesy Ray B. Lydston, Freeport, Maine.*

The great tower of Casco Castle during the fire of September, 1914, that destroyed the main building. This tower is all that remains today. *Courtesy Ray B. Lydston, Freeport, Maine.*

The stone tower of Casco Castle as it exists today is a guide to the mariner and a reminder of gay summer holidays long ago. *Courtesy Clifford Collins, Freeport, Maine.*

] 15 [

SEARLES CASTLE

THE SEARLES CASTLE, ALSO KNOWN AS THE STAN-ton-Harcourt Castle, is located near Windham, New Hampshire, where it is commonly referred to as The Castle. This magnificent, rambling structure is a one-quarter-size replica of the original celebrated Stanton-Harcourt Castle in Oxon County, England.

The Searles Castle was built by Edward F. Searles, who, as a young man, earned his living in the employment of an interior decorating company in New York. Acquaintances of Searles say he was a painter, but because of the firm he represented he was referred to as an interior decorator who was later to become a multi-millionaire, art connoisseur, and collector.

Searles was devotedly engaged in interior decoration, and in March, 1882, he visited the residence of the widowed Mrs. Mark Hopkins to examine her beautiful home and furnishings. Mrs. Hopkins, whose late husband was part owner of the Southern Pacific Railroad, had a keen aptitude for elaborate and expensive furniture, which Searles was interested in inspecting. This visit by the young man twenty-two years her junior, and the visits that followed, began a growing friendship and intimacy that resulted in their marriage four years later. Their relatively short marriage ended in July of 1891 when Mrs. Searles died, leaving her husband with the greater bulk of the estate. Her adopted son contested her will even though he received about ten million dollars, a smaller portion compared to that received by Mr. Searles.

Edward Searles later purchased over one thousand acres of beautiful countryside high in the delightful Southern New Hampshire area. With its panorama of wooded hills and surrounding mountains, the property included a frontage on Canobie Lake and Cobbets Pond. On top of one of the highest hills, Searles constructed a single-room cottage, while his less wealthy neighbor in nearby Methuen lived in a castle-type structure. The reason for Searles's wanting to build a castle is not entirely clear. He was a person known seldom to complete anything he started and enjoyed purchasing things at excessive prices that were in great demand or desired by others. Searles had grown somewhat eccentric and was also irritated at being accused of marrying for money rather than for love. It was not unusual for him to spend an entire day arranging furniture in a room. It was reported that upon entering a room he could instantly detect a misplaced object or piece of furniture, and would usually rearrange furnishings in a room until late at night. The next morning he would, more often than not, return the furnishings to their original positions.

When he decided to build his castle on the hill site near the cottage, Searles obtained the services of architect Irving Vaughn. Selecting the famous Stanton-Harcourt Castle as his model, Searles planned to build a smaller replica of the castle, sending the architect to England to draw reconstructed plans of the burned wing of the original castle. The model castle's coat of arms, though of no connecting family emblem, was still used as the official emblem for his castle.

Construction of the Searles Castle began in 1905 and was completed in 1912. The castle, of Tudor and medieval architecture, contains twenty principal rooms, including servants' quarters. Fine craftsmen, experts in their fields, were brought over from Europe to do the construction, exquisite carvings, and expert masonry found throughout the castle. Building materials had to be carried to the top of a nearby hill due to the peculiar location of the castle. An overhead trolley on cables was built from this hill to the castle hill site where workmen unloaded the supplies, which included Italian marble, oak, ivory, and mahogany. Stone for the imposing structure included dark-red sandstone and rough granite fieldstone, with eight-foot-thick foundation walls resting on deep bedrock.

The castle is essentially of three stories with four-foot-thick partitioned walls in the basement, which contained numerous large storage, laundry, and janitor rooms. At various exterior locations are several battlemented towers of rectangular and circular design with bastions and turrets at varying elevations. The principal rooms were a main reception hall, living room, music room, library, dining room, spacious, ivory-tinted tile kitchen, in addition to butler's pantry and storerooms, all on the first floor. The second floor contained the master suite with its large bedroom, marble fireplace, breakfast room, dressing room, and bath. There were two additional bedroom apartments, each with fireplaces and baths having doors that open to large, separate sun-porches that still offer a magnificent view. In the wing were three guest apartments with baths, in addition to maids' rooms and a linen room. The third floor was occupied by a great stateroom or ballroom finished in mahogany and ivory.

The castle is surrounded by a medieval-period granite stone wall eight feet thick at its base. Searles rebuilt portions of two roads, rerouting them away from the location of the new wall. Three miles of roadway wind throughout the estate, which has nine approaches to its main gates. Within the picturesque grounds are brooks, bridges, extensive woodlands, and attractive, well-attended gardens in the courtyard, which are still attractively maintained by present owners.

Of the many interesting features of this castle, a notable one is the traditional portcullis located inside the entrance and flanked by guard towers that are viewed from the courtyard. Unlike the old method of manually operating such a heavy gate, an automatic mechanism in one of the guard towers raises and lowers the portcullis with ease.

Within their beautiful, medieval setting, the varying heights and designs of the courtyard towers add interest to the castle. Reached by inner stairways, the tops of the towers offer panoramic views of the countryside in addition to the surrounding castle and grounds. In the largest tower a spiral staircase gives access to guest quarters, consisting of four rooms and bath. One tower, opposite the castle's main entrance, contains a flying staircase in which accurate balance and gravity are the only supports given to the ascending granite stair blocks.

The entrance hall, paneled in oak with tile floors, leads to the main reception hall, which is also paneled, with tiled floors and a ceiling of patterned timbers. The grand staircase displays magnificent wood carvings by creative craftsmen whose other work in ivory and mahogany is evident in several other rooms, such as the third-floor stateroom.

At the entrance to the living room are doors imported from Windsor Castle in England. Upon opening these doors the appealing living room reveals beautifully designed walls of hand-carved oak. As with several other balconies of the castle, the living room balcony is also expertly designed in hand-carved oak. The fireplace, inlaid in gold, was purchased at great expense by Searles, who obtained it from the Tuileries, royal palace in France. During unloading operations at the New York harbor, one of the fireplace's bases accidentally fell overboard. The lost base was replaced with one of similar dimensions but made of granite. France once tried to repurchase this fireplace from Searles, but owing to his peculiar nature of wanting things others desired, he refused to sell back his beautiful, fifty-thousand-dollar fireplace.

Like the library with its oak-paneled walls, the dining room walls are also paneled in oak with the added beauty of richly carved designs. The fireplace is of Italian marble, transported by a ship that sank, taking the fireplace with it to the depths of the sea. Several years later the fireplace was recovered and found to contain beautiful green and blue streaks in the marble caused by the action of the sea water.

The dining room ceiling is hand hewn in heavy timber. The windows are leaded and there is access to a hand-carved oak balcony.

A private reservoir on a nearby hilltop supplies pure, spring water to the castle. Present-day built-in baths and showers are incorporated into the bathrooms, which feature silver-plated plumbing fixtures with nickeled brass used in the piping. A steam-heating plant provides the convenience of efficiently heating the castle as a part of the modern refinements for added comfort. Other buildings on the estate include a twenty-room frame lodge, a nine-room brick farmhouse, a caretaker's cottage of six rooms, and an exceptionally large barn to accommodate carriages, harnesses, and grain rooms, plus numerous stalls.

Upon the death of Searles, the castle was left to his secretary, Mr. Walker, who did not occupy the castle for several years. When he finally sold his New York home and took permanent residence at the castle, his stay was destined to be a short one, for he died in the master bedroom of the castle within a week of his arrival.

In 1952 the castle was purchased by a Catholic religious order, the Sisters of Mercy, who still occupy and maintain this beautiful structure. Most of the land was sold, with 250 acres remaining as part of the castle grounds, which are enclosed by the high, stone parapet walls on the sides and a heavy, wire fence enclosing the fourth side of the property.

When Edward Searles built the castle he never completed it, leaving one of the towers unfinished. This tower was to contain a spiral stairway leading up to four guest rooms, none of which were built. Since the Sisters of Mercy have occupied the castle, they not only have completed this tower and joined it to the principal structure, but they have reproduced the architecture in a faithfully undetected manner, with the tower now being used as a chapel.

The setting and design of the Tudor and medieval architecture of the Searles Castle is strongly reminiscent of English castles and castellated estates. Such representation was achieved in this castle by the architect who faithfully created the effect that Searles desired and accomplished. The ivy-covered walls and towers of the castle have indeed captured the charm of noble medieval architecture of those far off, olden days when such picturesque castles once commanded the surrounding countryside.

The portcullis gate entry to the castle is flanked by guard towers. Though the castle was built in the 20th century, this view depicts a realistic medieval setting. *Courtesy F. J. Sullivan.*

The portcullis over this entrance to Searles Castle is lowered and raised by an automatic mechanism. *Courtesy F. J. Sullivan.*

Construction of Searles Castle, located near Windham, New Hampshire, was begun in 1905 and completed in 1912. *Courtesy F. J. Sullivan.*

] 16 [
RICHTHOFEN CASTLE

BARON WALTER VON RICHTHOFEN WAS BORN ON January 30, 1850,* in Kreisewitz, Silesia, Germany, on one of the estates of his father. He received his education in a school of cadets as did his six brothers. Taking leave for a year, he journeyed to New York in 1869, but returned to Germany in 1870 at the outbreak of the Franco-Prussian War. After the war he left the army and returned to the United States, where he took residence in Chicago for a time and was there during the Great Fire in October, 1871.

Baron von Richthofen later traveled to Denver, Colorado, where he gave language lessons in German, French, and Latin. In order to expand his knowledge of language he went to the Riviera to learn Italian, and it was there he met his first wife, English-born Jane Oakley. They were married in the early spring of 1878, in London, England, after which the Baron brought his wife to America, taking up residence in North Denver, Colorado. They had two daughters born in Denver, Margarethe, called Daisy, on December 28, 1878; and Charlotte, on March 19, 1882.

During the late 1870s and early 1880s, the Baron was active in promoting numerous projects in and around the young city of Denver, which was founded in 1858. Investing in South Denver real estate, he helped promote a local railroad service to that area,

giving easy access to people buying property there. He also built a beer garden, hoping to provide an enjoyment for families with imported beverages and band music. But the Baron's very respectable garden failed to attract the solid citizens who did not appreciate his efforts. Disgusted with the outcome of his efforts to bring some refinement to the people, he staged a one-night special, throwing the beer garden open to gamblers and ladies of ill repute. The long evening at the garden was a crowded and noisy success with many of the town's respectable men attending incognito.

In 1883 the family visited their relatives overseas. While there, Baron von Richthofen and his wife separated, with the Baron returning alone to Denver shortly thereafter. A divorce was later arranged after which the Baroness took residence in Germany, where she raised her two children.

In the years that followed, the Baron continued his active life of promoting various projects. In 1884 he met Mrs. Louise Ferguson Davies, whom he courted and later married in Denver on November 20, 1886. During this period prior to his second marriage, the Baron had an interest in cattle raising and wrote a book on the subject, which was published in 1885. In East Denver the Baron became extremely interested in a new town that was being developed, called Montclair. Through his efforts, he became the principal promoter in developing the area, and provided carriages and tallyhos for transporting pro-

---

* Dates of birth, death, and marriages are given according to the *Genealogisches Handbuch des Adels,* 1954.

spective buyers to Montclair.

During the mid-1880s, Baron von Richthofen decided to build a large, castellated mansion suitable for his bride, and fashioned, it is believed, similar to the von Richthofen home in Silesia. The castle was to be located on a 320-acre site in Montclair, once a separate entity, now a part of Denver. Large, hand-chiseled, gray stones, quarried at Castle Rock, south of Denver, were hauled to the site and used in the construction.

The battlemented structure, with its many lavishly furnished rooms, was two stories high, with a basement, two main towers, each three stories high, and an arched portico. A long, low wall fronted the castle, with main entrance gates of cast iron opening to a carriage driveway to the portico. Water was brought from Windsor Lake along an irrigation ditch, also called a moat, where the waterway ran on the castle grounds. West of the castle, a stone bridge was erected across the moat, with carved dates, 1887–1888, indicating the construction period of the castle, which the Baron called Louiseburgh.

The north main tower, with a battlemented roof perimeter, was rectangular, with its first floor at the arch main entry. Windows of the tower's second story were narrow and rectangular, while the third-story windows were arched at the top. Carved in the stone, north face of this tower, between the second and third stories, was the elaborate Richthofen lion and crown coat of arms. The west battlemented tower was circular in design as were the several ornate petite turrets rising from the corners of various walls. Immediately below the northwest petite corner turret and halfway up on the second story wall, was a handsomely carved, red-sandstone sculptured head representing Barbarossa, the twelfth century emperor of the Holy Roman Empire. As with the towers, much of the roof perimeter had battlements, though the structure today lacks these except over the portico.

The Baron acquired the services of a landscape gardener to improve the grounds, which the Baroness thought unattractive. Numerous trees were brought in from the East and Bear Creek Canyon, with profusions of flowers skillfully planted about the grounds. Flocks of wild canaries and numerous other songbirds were let loose on the estate, and several acres were fenced in to accommodate young deer, antelope, and other animals. With the landscaping

completed the Baron and his wife moved into the elegant castle in November of 1888, where they lived for three years.

During these years the Baron had other projects that kept him busy, one of which was the construction of a building near Montclair called the Molkerie, used as a sanatorium for health seekers. This two-story frame structure later became a civic center and had other uses throughout the years. The Baron also displayed paintings in Denver that he had collected while on trips to Europe. He later built an art gallery in Montclair to house and display the collection, and to bring some measure of culture to the primitive town of Denver. He had some success with this effort but the structure burned later in 1906.

Despite the efforts of the Baron to create pleasing and elegant surroundings of their home, the Baroness apparently was not accepted by the local social sets. Perhaps it was loneliness felt by the Baron's wife that prompted him to offer the castle for sale through a large advertisement placed in a Denver newspaper on January 24, 1891. In the spring of that year they left Denver, traveling to Mexico, California, and on a hunting trip to Alaska. They then departed for a European tour, finally settling in London, where they took residence in a Regent Street house. The Baron continued to receive income from real estate investments in Montclair until 1893, when the financial crash of that time caused payments to cease, including that of the castle, which he later repossessed. The Baron and Baroness returned to Denver in the mid-1890s, where he planned to convert Montclair properties into a great spa that would include baths and a large hotel.

Good progress was made with the spa, which had to be constructed outside the town limits due to objections of Montclair citizens. But this seeming success was not to last, for the Spanish-American War of 1898 ended many things for many people, including the Baron's flourishing spa. Having been a Prussian army officer, the Baron knew the meaning of war. In a patriotic manner he stood erect on the street, as soldiers of the United States Seventh Infantry paraded before leaving for duty, and he distributed well over one thousand bouquets of flowers to the passing soldiers.

At this time the Baron was in very poor health, and a few days later he underwent an operation that proved fatal when he died from shock on May 8,

1898, at the age of forty-eight. The Baron's funeral was held at a friend's home with many people attending the military interment given him. The Baroness spent the remaining thirty years of her life living in Denver hotels until she died on March 22, 1934. After the First World War the Baroness chose to be called simply Mrs. Richthofen, dropping her rightful title. Though the Baron loved America and was a patriotic man, he was also a valiant person, and no doubt, had he lived longer, he would have been proud of the daring feats of his nephew, Manfred Richthofen, a flying ace during World War I, who became known as the famous Red Knight of Germany.

Baroness von Richthofen sold the castle in 1903, and it was resold to Edwin Hendrie in the summer of that year. Hendrie called the structure Castlewood, and several years later, in 1910, he hired an architect to expand the building, adding a new wing, replacing the turrets and battlements, and making major revisions to the castle's interior. Beautifully designed timber and plaster walls were added above the first floor along with a well-adapted sloping English roof design, matching stone chimney shafts, and an expansion of the gatehouse. The detailed carved head of Barbarossa was carefully reset on another northeast corner of the new wing. In 1924 a new southwest wing and circular stairway were added by Hendrie, who occupied the structure until his death in 1932.

The hall of the remodeled interior has walls finished in bronze and gold leather with an imposing, dark-oak staircase leading to the second floor. The paneled, light-oak dining room and library, with ceiling-high bookcases, gives access through French doors to spacious porches. The long music room and adjoining reception room are most impressive, with walls of natural, finished beechwood. As with the dining room windows and music room windows, lead is used with the recessed windows that occupy an entire wall of the music room, each of which opens to the court. The second floor contains bedrooms, with marble fireplaces on both floors.

After the death of Mrs. Hendrie in 1937, this magnificent structure was sold by the heirs and resold by other owners over the years. Minor alterations were made after 1946, including the removal of numerous trees on the grounds, which were reduced in size when much of the land was sold. The water moat has long since been filled in and the old stone bridge removed, but the dated stones are inserted in the wall west of the main entry.

The estate is privately owned today. With the previous alterations made by Hendrie, the altered structure represents one of the finest examples of remodeled castles, with an agreeable balance of old and new architecture.

Baron Walter von Richthofen, 1850–1898. *Courtesy Denver Public Library Western Collection.*

Richthofen Castle, Denver, Colorado. The Baron's crest is seen on the square tower below the third-story windows. The carving of Barbarossa is on the corner of the second story to the right of the square tower. *Photo by William H. Jackson, courtesy Library, State Historical Society of Colorado.*

Richthofen Castle after alterations shows the pleasing combination of old architecture and half timber additions. *Photo by Louis C. McClure, courtesy Denver Public Library Western Collection.*

Front facade of Richthofen Castle after alterations. The circular drive leads to the main entry fronted by the stone terrace. *Photo by Louis C. McClure, courtesy Denver Public Library Western Collection.*

The Richthofen Castle after remodeling. The architecture to the right of the square has drastically changed from the old form but in a pleasing, well-adapted manner. The head of Barbarossa was moved to the corner, seen in the lower right of the photograph. *Photo by Orin A. Sealy, courtesy Denver Public Library Western Collection.*

] 17 [

CHATEAU LAROCHE

CHATEAU LAROCHE, LOCATED AT LOVELAND, OHIO, is a unique structure of one man's efforts and ability to erect with his own hands an expression in architecture of the rugged grandeur that existed when knighthood was in flower. Harry D. Andrews began work on his castle on June 5, 1929, and he continues with its construction today, almost forty years later, at the time of this writing.

Andrews was born at Oneonta, New York, on April 5, 1890. He attended Colgate University at Hamilton, New York, where he studied Greek, Roman, and Egyptian architecture, and graduated there in 1916. He later took two years of graduate work at Pennsylvania University, and an additional two years of study at Cincinnati University in Ohio. During World War I, Andrews served in the medical corps and the intelligence service. After the war he remained in France and studied at Toulouse University, one of his subjects being Norman architecture, which he later used as a basis for planning Chateau Laroche.

Andrews taught Sunday school in Cleveland, Ohio, and in 1927 he purchased some land near a small river where his class of young men could have a place for recreation and set up tents for camping. Since the original purchase of land, several additional lots were added, amounting to about one and one half acres on which the castle now stands. After the tents had been used for nearly three years they began to decay. Andrews suggested that the boys

fetch stones and he would build them a stone shelter. Two small rooms were constructed and used for camping during one summer. These same two rooms today form the bottom of the two towers that face the river. During the depression of that time several of the homeless boys went to the Civilian Conservation Corps and very few people came regularly to the early beginnings of the castle for the next three years. The depression having relaxed somewhat, Andrews continued construction work on the structure with the aid of several of the boys who had no home other than his. Since that time, with the exception of incidental help from visitors and friends, Andrews worked completely alone on the castle's construction. Donations of sand, cement, and other materials helped in the early stages of the castle development.

The Second World War brought a period of almost two years delay in construction due to rationing and lack of cement. Andrews was able to work on the structure an average of only slightly more than one hour per week during the first twenty-five years of the castle's construction.

After about thirty years of teaching Sunday school, he relinquished that part of his activities and gave his full attention to construction of the castle. Until 1952 the materials, tools, and other supplies were sledded down a hill in back of the castle, since there was no road leading to the site of construction. Andrews and some neighbors constructed a rough road along what is now called Mulberry Street, and later the county put a black surface on that section. Andrews then began the laborious task of personally carrying some four thousand pailfuls of stone to make a foundation for a road to the castle. Later in 1958 county road officials agreed to take over this piece of road and maintain it.

In May, 1955, Andrews retired from his employment with the Standard Publishing Company. At the end of that same month he moved into the Dome Room, the first major part of the castle to be completed. Living in this one-room shelter was difficult with only the heat of his wood-fed fireplace for warmth in the cold grip of winter. But construction began moving more rapidly after that. Handmade piping for the drains and sewers were cast lengthwise, in halves, forming in a half-jointed, overlapping manner. The castle dimensions were to be approximately ninety-six by sixty-five feet. Due to the weight of the structure, the walls were laid directly on rock in the ground with no artificial foundation. Drainage piping for excess water was laid under the castle. Other drains were laid to take the surface water from the nearby hillside.

A dungeon, with its two cells and thirty-inch walls, was also constructed and is now the official neighborhood bomb shelter, and for now the dungeon serves as storage for home-canned foods. An alcove in the dungeon now holds an oil-burning furnace for supplying heat to all the other rooms throughout the castle. A pump is located in a small room under the stairs that lead to the dungeon. This pump draws drinking water from an eighty-foot-deep well located in the courtyard north of the castle. The brick used in the structure was made by filling some thirty-two thousand quart-size milk cartons with concrete.

The main floor contains the living room, the kitchen, and a small office, in addition to the tower stairways. The kitchen walls are covered with handmade cement tiles and though not a large room, it has ten windows. The floor is uniquely constructed for insulation against dampness with one thousand quart-size oil cans laid on top of two inches of a dry mix. Concrete was then poured over the cans, giving a total thickness of fourteen inches.

The large living room with its overhead concrete beams is located over the dungeon. Beneath the windows at sill height around the room is a narrow shelf known as the sword shelf, where knights could leave their swords in readiness for instant use. Beside the fireplace with its unusual draft is the Andrews family coat of arms.

The main entrance door also opens onto this floor and is heavily constructed of 233 pieces of wood in three layers. The door is also studded with more than twenty-five hundred nails for added strength. Such nail studded doors were use in medieval times as a protection against an invader's axe.

The third floor contains a larger room than the living room space on the main floor, and is lined with concrete bricks. There is also a bay window to diffuse entering sunlight throughout the room. A concrete balcony is also located on this level with a floor and overhead roof strengthened with five steel cables in each section. A wall-bolted ladder leads from the floor to a small room under the highest tower. The second corner tower contains bathroom facilities. A curved stairway in the northwest corner of this floor leads up to the roof, a flat, concrete area surrounded by breast-high walls topped with eighty-eight battlements.

The castle banner, unfurled on Sundays, is a handmade combination of various banners used by the ancient crusaders. A 220-foot retaining wall, ten feet high and two feet thick, was constructed with a thirteen-step stairway leading up to the road through a stone, arched gateway. Located to the right of the gateway at the retaining wall is an underground garage. The retaining wall is said to contain as many stones as the entire castle itself.

In addition to terraces with hotbeds and flower beds, a small orchard was planted on the hillside with various fruit trees and grape and berry vines.

Andrews has spent many thousands of hours in labor on the construction of his remarkable castle. Such an undertaking by one made has not been easy, but with his faith and persistent determination the work continues with several additions planned for the future. Andrews has also found time to write poetry under the pen name of Harry N. Drews. To Harry Andrews, Chateau Laroche represents not only his home and family, but a reminder of those far off days of chivalry and armor-clad knights. And, with the passing of time, it will also one day be his monument.

Chateau Laroche, with towers and battlements and rows of similarly designed windows. Mr. Andrews is pictured at the left. *Courtesy Dayton Daily News.*

Harry Andrews in an early period of construction on Chateau Laroche. *Courtesy Harry D. Andrews.*

Harry Andrews at work on the castle he has been constructing since 1929. *Courtesy Dayton Daily News.*

Chateau Laroche in the grip of winter. The retaining
wall and underground garage are recent additions.
Courtesy Harry D. Andrews.

One of the rugged corner towers of Chateau Laroche.
Courtesy Harry D. Andrews.

] 18 [
WALKER CASTLE

IN THE EARLY 1860S A WEALTHY ENGLISHMAN named Benjamin Walker journeyed from England to Madison, Wisconsin, with his wife, two young daughters, and son. He acquired extensive property along Lake Mendota on which he soon proceeded to erect a towered, Norman structure as a home for his family. The actual date of construction of his castellated structure, known as Walker's Castle, is not entirely clear, but it is believed to be within the period of 1861 to 1863. County title reports indicate that Walker acquired the property in 1861, the same year he arrived in Madison, where he went into partnership for a short time in the bookbinding and stationery business.

The castle, built of native sandstone, was erected on a small hill adjoining Lake Mendota. Walker designed the castle on a plan that called for battlemented towers, arched, Gothic doorways and windows, and accouterments based on a small medieval castle. The four corners of the overall structure were occupied by circular towers, two small, lower towers, and two higher, battlemented towers that flanked the main, front, stone entrance porch. These outer towers were connected by a stone parapet wall, high in the front of the building and low on the two sides and rear. A curved drive once led to the small, front porch that was raised, like the balance of the structure, on slightly higher ground above the drive and stone-walled lawn that sloped down to the lake. A two-story, square, battlemented building, faced with arched windows, was located within the perimeter of the towers and walls. This centrally located building was connected by adjoining smaller buildings at both the front and rear of the structure.

The rough, stone blocks used in construction were well adapted both in workmanship and appearance of the circular towers and square main building. Wide-spaced battlements of the central, two-story main building were placed on top of only two opposite walls, but the decorative frieze bordered all four sides. The rear, circular corner towers contained vertical gun slots with round view openings at the ends. All windows of the castle had deep-casemented windows of various widths but of similar heights. Above the main entrance door and centered between battlements a shield was placed, resembling what may have been the family's coat of arms.

With a stone barn and stables to the rear, the main building's interior consisted of parlors, study, sitting room, dining room, kitchen, and bedrooms. On opposite sides of the large entrance hall, and located within the circumference of the two front towers, were two similar octagonal parlors papered in gold. Both of these rooms contained fireplaces constructed of white marble with intricately carved designs of grape clusters and vines. The crimson color of the deep carpets was also used in the upholstery of the heavy furnishings of the parlor on the right, while the carpets and furnishings of the left parlor were done in green. Heavy, gold frames held large oil paintings that adorned the walls of both parlors. Much of the furnishings were brought from England, such as the heavy, oak furniture of the dining room, which was located, as was the kitchen, below the living room. Evening meals were served here on excellent chinaware by the light of candles mounted on silver candelabras.

There was an underground passageway that led from the castle to the stables. Years later this same passageway was used for fraternity initiation stunts where a night expedition through the deserted cobwebbed tunnel provided a frightening and lurid experience for trembling freshmen. But during Walker's residence the tunnel proved to be a handy and dry passage in bad weather. On fine, sunny days the Walkers' glass-enclosed cabriolet, with green trimmings, could be seen rolling through the woods as the coachman on the driver's box led the horses up the curving drive by the lake to the castle entrance.

Mrs. Walker is described as a pleasant little Englishwoman, with soft, brown hair and blue eyes, who took great pleasure and spent much time in romping and playing with her children. Mr. Walker was somewhat of a mysterious, silent man who made few friends and spent much of his time in his study in one of the towers. His outings in the cabriolet did not include the rest of his family, and he apparently seldom took meals with them.

The Walkers' stay in America was to extend only a few years. In 1866 the castle was sold, after which the family packed their belongings and returned to England. The new owners of the castle found the place to be damp and difficult to heat to their satisfaction. In the following years the property passed into several hands, and one of the last purchasers of the castle left it vacant for several years. During this period the structure fell into a state of ruin. The roof leaked, windows were broken, and the big empty rooms became heavy with the musty odor of decay. It was during this time that the castle obtained a reputation of being haunted by a ghost, a belief that stuck with many local citizens for quite some time.

Finally, in 1893 this forlorn and deteriorating castle home, once part of a picturesque setting by the lake, was torn down. Located at a lower level near the lake, the stone barn that was built of similar materials and resembled the main building, was not razed at the time but survived the castle for many decades. Standing some distance from the castle this fifty-foot-square structure once housed the Walkers' fine cabriolet and horses. It had small, narrow, Gothic windows, gables, and wide double doors.

The stone blocks of the castle were carted away and used in the building of a modern house of the times. The grounds were divided into two properties and sold. Thus ended the relatively short, thirty-year existence of the Walker Castle, which today remains only as a memory.

Walker Castle, from a lithograph by Louis Kurz.
Courtesy State Historical Society of Wisconsin.

Walker Castle, from a lithograph by Louis Kurz.
Courtesy State Historical Society of Wisconsin.

Walker Castle, about 1880 to 1885. *Photo by F. W. Curtiss, courtesy State Historical Society of Wisconsin.*

Walker Castle, about 1885 to 1890. *Courtesy State Historical Society of Wisconsin.*

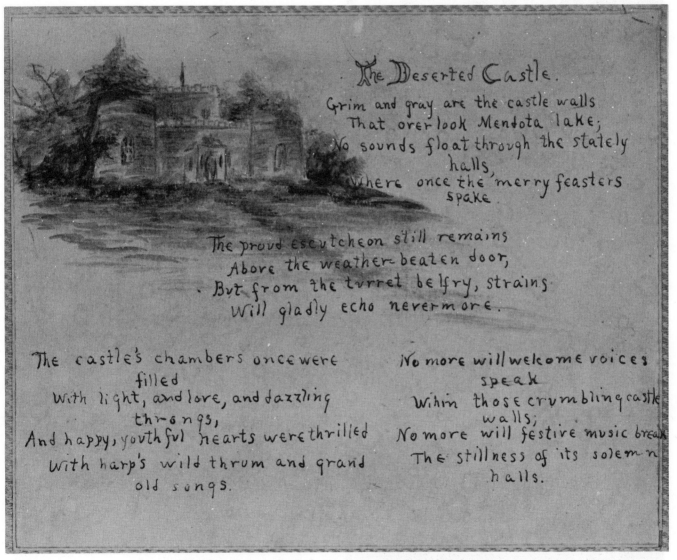

The Deserted Castle.

Grim and gray are the castle walls
That over look Mendota lake;
No sounds float through the stately
              halls,
Where once the merry feasters
              spake.

The proud escutcheon still remains
Above the weather-beaten door,
But from the turret belfry, strains
Will gladly echo nevermore.

The castle's chambers once were
              filled
With light, and love, and dazzling
              throngs,
And happy, youthful hearts were thrilled
With harp's wild thrum and grand
              old songs.

No more will welcome voices
              speak
Within those crumbling castle
              walls;
No more will festive music break
The stillness of its solemn
              halls.

Sketch and poem by Isabella A. Dengel, who lived near
Walker Castle during the 1890s. *Courtesy State Historical Society of Wisconsin.*

Walker Castle, front elevation. *Courtesy State Historical Society of Wisconsin.*

Walker Castle, rear door. *Photo by Frederick K. Conover, courtesy State Historical Society of Wisconsin.*

Walker Castle, rear elevation. *Photo by Frederick K. Conover, courtesy State Historical Society of Wisconsin.*

] 19 [

INGELSIDE

A FINE EXAMPLE OF MEDIEVAL GOTHIC ARCHITEC-
ture was the structure known as Ingelside, formally
located at Lexington, Kentucky, and built by Joseph
Bruen, a prosperous owner of a brass and iron
foundry. He journeyed to Europe in 1841 with two
of his five daughters and the builder, John McMurty.
The visit was to make a study of Europe's Gothic-
style architecture and to give the builder some idea
of what Bruen wanted his future home to look like.

In 1843 Bruen purchased about three hundred
acres of land south of the city of Lexington where
he intended to erect a Gothic-style structure that was
to be a gift for his eldest daughter, Elizabeth, who
in 1837 married Henry Brook Ingels, a great
nephew of Daniel Boone. Construction was soon begun on the castellated structure. John McMurty
based his design on his studies of and inspirations
from his extensive European journeys.

Bruen died in 1848, several years before the structure was completed, with Ingels taking charge of the
foundry's operations for the widow. He also saw to
the completion of Ingelside and may have had much
to do with certain details of its construction.

Stone was obtained from a nearby quarry and the
numerous bricks were pressed on the site of construction. Much of the interior trim and other timber construction was obtained from trees felled
on the property. The Bruen foundry provided the
cast-iron sills, pinnacles, window and doorway drip-
molds, and a few other cast-iron details, some of

which might normally have been constructed in
stone for this type of structure. After a long period of
construction, amounting to nearly a decade, Ingelside
was finally completed in 1852.

Ingelside has been compared to another similar
structure built near Lexington, Kentucky, called
Loudoun, whose architect was Alexander Jackson
Davis. This structure, however, was not started until
Ingelside was well along in its construction. Mc-
Murty was also the builder of Loudoun and worked
from plans designed by Davis.

Ingelside was of an L-shape design, two stories
high with several three-story, battlemented towers,
the majority of which were located on the south
principal facade. A portico entrance led to a central
hall with a large dining room and parlor on either
side. Other rooms within the longer wing portion of
the L on the first floor included a library, dining
room, service rooms, kitchen, hallways and staircases
to the second floor. Angled on two rear walls of the
building was a long veranda with an entrance to the
central hall. The second floor contained sleeping
chambers, some of which made use of the corner
turrets as closets. Each of these upper chambers also
had its own fireplace, which accounted for the many
chimneys rising from various positions on the roof.
Upper staircases, bath, and hallways, made up the
remainder of this second floor.

The extreme rear of this wing contained the
kitchen and service rooms. The chamber above, on

the second floor, had a roof elevation lower than the remainder of the building. The windows of this section were plain and rectangular, in great contrast to the narrow, arched windows with their diamond-shaped panes on the principal portion of the structure. Spanning the width of the kitchen and adjoining hall, a small, covered porch had access to this rear hall and may have been used as a receiving entrance for foodstuffs.

All four towers of Ingelside extended one story above the principal building walls. The smaller, octagonal corner towers appeared to be much higher than they were, perhaps due to their slender shape with narrow windows in each, located on the second and third stories. The main tower was several feet higher and of larger area than the three corner towers. Cornered between the library and parlor on the first floor and two chambers of the second floor, the main tower contained diamond-paned, Gothic windows on each of its three stories. One chamber of the second floor made use of its portion of this tower as a dressing room, while the lower portion was exposed to the parlor as an alcove.

The windows of the principle portion of Ingelside were arched with diamond-shaped, stained-glass panes, which were also found in the doors of the drawing room leading to the rear veranda. The parlor alcove, library, and dining room had window shutters that folded back into casings that projected slightly into these rooms. Centered between two towers was the drawing room bay window, which was also centered within the drawing room and opposite to the semicircular, arched fireplace with its white-marble mantel. Fireplaces were also found in the parlor, library, and dining room, with mantels of marbelized iron.

A crisscross-patterned, beamed ceiling extended the full length of the center hall. Tall, glass-paneled double doors at opposite ends of the hall provided direct access from the main entrance through to the rear veranda. The interior doors were of walnut and cherry wood, some with carvings in narrow spandrel panels.

Projecting from a second-story chamber located above the library was an oriel window, which was the greatest point of projection in that entire wall facade, providing a fine, unobstructed view. The rooms on the second-story were not on an equal level as were those on the first floor. Above the kitchen and serving areas of the first floor, the bed-

room, bath, and passages were on a lower level than the other chambers and halls of the principal portion of the building. Two small sets of steps, one in the hall and another leading to the chamber above the dining room, provided access to the two levels of the second story.

An octagonal, brick smokehouse was once located behind the kitchen wing but was removed in 1938. Servants quarters were also located farther back of the principal building in the form of a cottage with six rooms, three of which were on the second floor.

After Ingel's death, Ingelside was sold in 1868 to Colonel J. Watts Kearney, who later built a castellated, brick gatehouse at the entrance to the castle. The entering front face of this battlemented structure was two stories high with rectangular windows and a battlemented wall perimeter whose corner merlons served as chimneys. A wrought-iron gate opened to the carriageway that passed through the center of the structure. A sloping shed roof joined the upper front story and sloped down to the rear first-story level, covering the gatehouse rooms and spanning the carriageway as one complete roof section. Once through the gatehouse the drive wound through the wooded grounds to the portico of the picturesque castellated structure of Ingelside.

The property was owned by successive owners after Colonel Kearney. In the late 1880s Ingelside was the scene of much entertainment with many distinguished guests, such as Theodore Roosevelt.

Years ago the gatehouse was enlarged and converted into an apartment house when the front property was portioned off into building lots. Since then Ingelside was drastically altered into apartments, and in the 1940s lots were used as a trailer camp. Ingelside and its six and one half surrounding acres were purchased in 1961 and scheduled to become a part of the expanding trailer-park development. The small house at the rear of the main building, once occupied by servants, was torn down in 1963, and in 1964 the main structure of Ingelside was dismantled to provide additional trailer space for the park.

Ingelside was one of the great, distinguished structures of its type in Kentucky. Its combined Gothic and turreted architecture presented an exotic and picturesque setting of Old-World charm etched in the memory of John McMurty when he journeyed to foreign lands where such architecture is the nations' historic and cherished treasure.

Ingelside, at Lexington, Kentucky, showing circular
drive to front entrance. The towers and Gothic architecture of this castellated structure are defined in this
photo taken in the summer of 1940. *Photo by Lester
Jones, from collections of the Library of Congress.*

Window detail of Ingelside showing variations in design. *Photo by Lester Jones, ca. 1940, from the collections of the Library of Congress.*

Gothic and bay window detail. *Photo by Lester Jones, ca. 1940, from the collections of the Library of Congress.*

Detail of the octagonal tower. *Photo by Lester Jones, ca. 1940, from the collections of the Library of Congress.*

Ingelside, showing rear porch and corner veranda. Some of the twin chimney shafts are viewed. *Photo by Lester Jones, ca. 1940, from the collections of the Library of Congress.*

Detail of corner veranda at Ingelside. *Photo by Lester Jones, ca. 1940, from the collections of the Library of Congress.*

] 20 [
HUNDRED OAKS CASTLE

ARTHUR HADLY MARKS COMPLETED HIS SCHOOL-ing in 1882 at the age of seventeen at Sewanee, Tennessee. He read law in the office of his father, Albert S. Marks, Tennessee's twenty-first governor and son of a member of the Lewis and Clark expedition.

In 1888 Arthur Marks was appointed to the counselor service of the American legation under President Cleveland. Gladly accepting the position, which gave him the opportunity of visiting the Old World, he proceeded to London. He spent many months traveling over the English and Scottish countryside admiring the many castles dotted throughout the land.

Arthur Marks later obtained a transfer to Berlin, where he met Miss Mary Hunt, a wealthy girl he had known in Nashville, Tennessee. Resigning from the counselor service, he journeyed to Stirling, Scotland, where he and Miss Hunt were married that November. After touring several countries in Europe, Marks and his bride returned to the United States in February of 1889. They settled in Winchester, Tennessee, where they took up residence in a large, two-story, brick house owned by Marks's father. The house was situated on approximately six hundred acres of land and was said to have one hundred oaks on it, thus the estate's name, Hundred Oaks.

Shortly after settling at Hundred Oaks, Marks sought to improve the plain, rectangular house with ideas inspired by his European travels. He began drawing plans for a castellated mansion that was to incorporate many features he had admired in European castles. His plans called for many additional rooms, including a ballroom, portrait gallery, library, carriage house, wine cellars, aviary, and many other traditional additions such as corbiestepped gables, cloisters, and towers.

Construction work was begun in 1889 with bricks pressed and baked at the site and stones hauled down the mountain from Sewanee. As great, double walls began to rise, trees were felled to provide for the wood-paneled interiors. Wings went out to enclose a courtyard and from the roof appeared a number of high chimneys. On one corner of the structure a five-story battlemented tower was erected. Circular battlemented towers of various elevations were raised, as were others topped with low pitched conical roofs. Wells were dug, refilled, and dug again to suit the critical eye of Arthur Marks, who watched his ideas take their form. No expense was spared in the project, which took nearly three years.

Exterior, columned, supported arches made up the long arcade on one face of the main structure on the first and second floors adjoining the main towers. Arched windows were found on all faces of the building, many of which were made up of small, rectangular panes of glass. Thousands of bricks were used in the construction of this all-brick castle, creating an interesting effect in its design, particularly in the small circular towers. Another interesting feature is that of the gables with their small, pyramidal roof peaks that extend over the windows. Viewing the strange combination of various attached structures that make up the castle, it is easy to conceive how the interior rooms could vary considerably both in design and dimension. A variety of ceiling designs were found throughout the castle, such as the forty-five-foot-high arched ceiling of the picture gallery, also used in later years by Paulist Fathers as a chapel. A square-patterned, wood-beamed ceiling was found above one of the hallways, where neat rows of wood balusters made up the staircase leading to the upper floors.

Grapevines imported from France and ivy transplanted from Sir Walter Scott's home at Abbotsford, all became a part of what Arthur considered essential to the gracious life of Old-World leisure. The estate now had all the conveniences of a modern home of the times combined with the stateliness and grandeur of an English castle. The library was constructed as a replica of Sir Walter Scott's. There were sitting rooms, dining rooms, kitchens, small tower rooms, and at least a dozen bedrooms. By 1892 the structure had become one of the most imposing and stately edifices of Tennessee. But the castle was never really completed in detail. Marks abandoned practicing law and began a baronial life of an English country gentleman. His time was spent in attending to the installations at Hundred Oaks and in writing and contemplation. The life of leisure at the castle was not destined to last since Marks had little talent for administering the estate. His failure to understand money and his carefree attitude toward the large expenses soon resulted in the dissipation of family funds.

About a year after his father passed away, Marks, his wife, Mary, and their little son visited his mother in Monteagle. While there, Marks fell sick of typhoid fever and died at the very young age of twenty-eight, on September 7, 1892. Mary Marks stayed on at Hundred Oaks for nearly a year, then married an attorney. Arthur's brother, Albert Marks, managed to assemble some of the writings of his deceased brother, which were later published in a handsome volume entitled *Igerne and Other Writings of Arthur Hadly Marks*.

Hundred Oaks passed into judicial custody and was finally sold by court order. It was resold again in 1900 to Paulist Fathers of New York, who occupied it for over fifty years.

In the monastic atmosphere of Hundred Oaks, the thirty-room castle was admirably suited for a monastery providing spaciousness and seclusion. During the conversion of Hundred Oaks from a country estate to monastery, the Paulist Fathers sold all but twenty-five acres of the land, applying the proceeds to the renovation and adaptation of the building, which they renamed the House of St. Francis de Sales. The forty-four-foot-long ballroom, rising two stories high, was converted into a chapel. By midsummer of 1900, Paulist community life was established at the castle. As the years passed the castle became the nerve center of a large parish that embraced some fourteen counties.

The estate was used by this missionary order as a Southern headquarters until 1954. Since then, the property has changed hands several times and for a time was abandoned and subject to deterioration and vandalism with some damage to the exterior. The neglected castle creation of the poetic Arthur Marks still stands and at present is privately owned. The present owners intend to improve the property and make it their home.

The feudal charm of Hundred Oaks Castle remains as a monument to the young Arthur Marks whose dreams of castles long ago were realized at Hundred Oaks.

Hundred Oaks Castle as it exists today is a combination of turrets, towers, and battlements built entirely of brick. *Photo by Ann Ford, Winchester, Tennessee.*

The second floor balcony is fronted by a series of columned arches with broad arched openings of similar design on the floor below. The gabled windows are typical of numerous others found throughout the castle. *Photo by Ann Ford, Winchester, Tennessee.*

Detail of the second floor columned arches. *Photo by Ann Ford, Winchester, Tennessee.*

The portico, with its high arched openings, features battlements and buttress supports. *Photo by Ann Ford, Winchester, Tennessee.*

The main octagonal tower rises above the entire castle with views of the surrounding area provided through its arched square-paned windows. *Photo by Ann Ford, Winchester, Tennessee.*

Round tower showing window detail. Though windows vary in dimension, their design is uniform with square glass panes dominating. *Photo by Ann Ford, Winchester, Tennessee.*

The interesting peaked gable windows at the upper left are numerous throughout the castle as are the high unusual brick chimney pieces. *Photo by Ann Ford, Winchester, Tennessee.*

High peaked roofs of corner turrets have a similarity to the peaked gables in their style. The stepped window to the right of the corner turret is an indication of the stairs within. *Photo by Ann Ford, Winchester, Tennessee.*

Detail of small, conical roofed turrets. Weather and vandalism have taken their toll over the years of this castle estate. *Photo by Ann Ford, Winchester, Tennessee.*

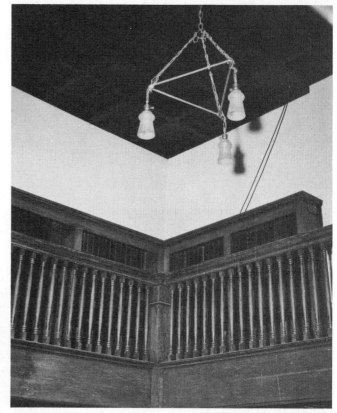

Detail of landing balusters and beamed ceiling. *Photo by Ann Ford, Winchester, Tennessee.*

Stair window detail. *Photo by Ann Ford, Winchester, Tennessee.*

Circular tower window detail showing framing and a portion of the beam ceiling construction. *Photo by Ann Ford, Winchester, Tennessee.*

The high arched ceiling extends the full length of this room. A portion of the upper wood molding is shown at its termination at the base of the ceiling. *Photo by Ann Ford, Winchester, Tennessee.*

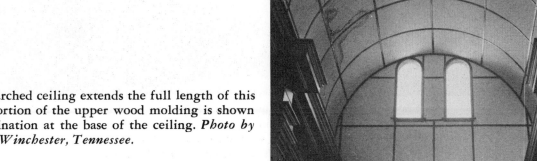

The great hall was once used as a chapel by Paulist Fathers. Wood beam columns rise at intervals to the broad wood-molded frieze separating the wall and beginning of the high arched ceiling. *Photo by Ann Ford, Winchester, Tennessee.*

] 21 [

SCOTTY'S CASTLE

WALTER PERRY SCOTT WAS BORN IN 1872, AT Cynthiana, Kentucky. His father was a breeder of racehorses and a distiller in the vicinity of Lexington. During his early childhood, Scotty's mother died, and he never received a formal education. Before he was in his teens, he borrowed money from his brother and journeyed by train to Nevada. In Humboldt Wells, he obtained a thirty-dollar-a-month job as a horse wrangler in the employ of John Sparks, who was later to become governor of Nevada.

When Scotty was about twelve years old, he was hired on one of Death Valley's twenty-mule-team outfits hauling borax to Mohave from the Old Harmony Works. He later took a job as water boy for a survey party that was doing survey work in the valley. Among the personnel of this party he met some of the old-time prospectors, who gave him the "gold fever" that was to stay with him the rest of his life. Scotty drifted back to Humboldt Wells after the survey party broke up, taking a job as a horse wrangler again. During this time the sheep war became very bitter, and so he moved on to Idaho. He had by this time become an expert rider and bronco buster. Some scouts from the Buffalo Bill Wild West Show came to purchase wild horses that Scotty and a friend had been wrangling. But the scouts were unable to handle the wild broncs and the purchase of the animals was about to fall through. An arrangement was made so that Scotty and his friend would go along to handle the horses. This then became the prelude to Scotty's career as a showman with the Buffalo Bill show. His knowledge of horses and his riding skill soon became apparent to Buffalo Bill, who made him a feature rider along with the star of the show, Annie Oakley.

He stayed with the show for eleven years during which time leaders of society and men of wealth sought his acquaintance. By now Scotty was a grown man, strong, and with the intelligence to meet and converse with these people. Though he was an entertaining talker, he never took advantage of this society, since such influence and wealth meant nothing to him then. He wanted to save his money and return to Death Valley to find the gold mine he often thought of. When the show was in winter quarters, Scotty wandered throughout the West and was one of the first on the ground when Goldfield was discovered, but he never staked a claim.

In New York, just before the turn of the century, Walter Scott met Josephine Millius on a blind date. Some time later, in 1900, they were married. After he left the show, Scotty decided to give his full time to prospecting. While in New York, he went to see Mr. Julian Gerard, then vice-president of the Knickerbocker Trust Company, whom he had met while riding with the show. When their meeting was ended, Scotty had signed a fifty-fifty grubstake contract without bothering to read the fine print. After prospecting in Death Valley for three years, Scotty returned to New York to report to Gerard that he had failed after spending some eight thousand dollars of Gerard's money. Later, as time passed, Scotty had the money to repay his debt to Gerard, but the man refused to accept it and instead wanted claim to half of Scotty's mine when he located one. The troubles between Scotty and Gerard lasted for a long time with Gerard's agents trailing Scotty for many years after. Scotty roamed all over Death Valley and knew it as well as any old-time prospector. His adventures in the West are well known, as is the fantastic legend of a mine that saw him rise from a stake puncher to the wild, money spender on sprees in Los Angeles, and other places where he was to become known as Death Valley Scotty.

It later became generally known that Scotty's association with Albert Johnson, a Chicago millionaire, may have had some connection with Scotty's "mine." Scotty had urged Johnson to join him in Death Valley, where Johnson's poor health could benefit from the climate of pure air and sunshine. Johnson attributed his regained health to Scotty, and they formed a partnership that was to last for the remainder of their lifetime.

It was in 1925 that rumors started coming from Death Valley that Scotty was constructing a castle near the upper end of the valley at Grapevine Canyon, some three thousand feet above sea level. Actually, construction on the castle started in 1924 alongside the shack where Johnson had regained his health. The idea for the castle developed one day when Scotty and Johnson were at Scotty's desert camp. Resting in the desert heat, Scotty was daydreaming with wishful thinking for a castle like those he had seen along the Rhine while visiting Europe during his days with the Buffalo Bill show. Johnson instantly approved of the idea and thus the castle had its beginnings.

The style of the castle is perhaps best described as a combination of Moorish, Spanish, and Italian architecture. Plans called for twelve bathrooms, kitchens, living room, dining room, and music room, in addition to several other rooms and tunnels under the castle that extended from the powerhouse to the guest house, carrying power lines as well as water and sewage lines. A high watchtower was also to be built, with twenty-five large chimes that could be heard for miles around. Large clocks are located on all four sides of the tower, with each clock face several feet in diameter.

Hundreds of workmen were on the job laying the huge foundations and high walls. Water from the Grapevine Spring would provide for six hundred gallons per minute, sufficient to run the generators and fill the planned 185-foot-long swimming pool. Materials were trucked over the then primitive roads, since the nearest railroad was many miles away. Austrian and Spanish wood-carvers were recruited to create the massive, hand-carved beams and hand-wrought metal. In spite of the problems of transportation and labor, several work crews kept on the job, and the two-storied structure soon began to take its shape. The kitchen's tiles were brought from Spain, and a large walk-in refrigerator was installed that could hold a month's supply of food.

Built of concrete and roofed with red tile, the main building has two units on opposite sides of an oblong patio. Both units have towers, one of which is topped with a wrought-iron weathervane showing Scotty driving burros on the trail. The living room is a vast, two-storied chamber that occupies much of the main building, with a large fireplace at one end and a fountain at the other. From the interior balcony that overhangs this room are guest rooms that are designed and furnished in the grand manner with characteristics similar to prerevolutionary Spain.

Irreplaceable rugs were made on the island of Majorca especially for the castle, and tiles for the pool and other areas were imported from the Mediterranean. Many of the furnishings were brought from cathedrals and palaces of Morocco and Spain. Draperies made for the castle were hand-tooled in selected sheepskin leather. Sixty hand-carved panels, each of different design, were installed in the music-room ceiling. A Welte Mignon organ reported to have cost 160,000 dollars, and the finest instrument of its kind in the West, was located in this music room. Though Scotty could not play this instrument, world-famous musicians who stayed at the castle years later gave private concerts for Scotty and his friends.

Scotty also purchased fifteen hundred dollars worth of railroad ties of an abandoned run of track, and spent another twenty-five thousand dollars to have the ties gathered and shipped to the castle to be used as firewood.

Approximately some two million dollars was spent on the castle, presumably from Scotty's "gold mine." At first the placed was called the Johnson and Scott Ranch, with a J-S brand. But with Scotty's dramatic flare, he called it a castle, and it was soon to become widely known as Scotty's Castle.

Scotty and Johnson both derived immense enjoyment from this desert castle, which was finished long before the death of both men. After Johnson died in 1948, Scotty spent a great deal of time at the castle spinning yarns for the tourists and posing for pictures. Scotty died in 1954, over eighty years of age. He had become a legend in his own lifetime, though the true story of Death Valley Scotty may never be written, since the fine line between fact and fiction is difficult to draw even for those who were close to him. But in the world's most unlikely spot, in Death Valley, his monument stands, the desert dwelling of Scotty's Castle.

Death Valley Scotty's Castle is located in Grapevine Canyon at the north end of Death Valley, California. *Courtesy Union Pacific Railroad.*

Scotty's Castle is a mixture of Spanish, Italian, and Moorish architecture. The castle offers rooms, good meals, and is filled with art objects and antiques gathered from everywhere. *Courtesy Union Pacific Railroad.*

Scotty's Castle in Grapevine Canyon. The large swimming pool pictured in the lower center was never completed. *Courtesy Union Pacific Railroad.*

Hourly sight-seeing trips are conducted through Scotty's Castle, a palatial home occupied once by the colorful Scotty, who once hired a special train to make a record-breaking trip on the Santa Fe from Los Angeles to Chicago. *Photo by R. C. Bradley, courtesy Santa Fe Railway.*

Death Valley Scotty and his wife. *Courtesy Santa Fe Railway.*

Death Valley Scotty told many a tale of his adventurous youth. For 50 years he continued to make the headlines of newspapers across the nation. In 1905 he started scattering gold nuggets and $100 dollar bills from New York to Los Angeles. *Courtesy Union Pacific Railroad.*

Death Valley Scotty with his pets. He remained at the castle during the twilight years of his life. *Courtesy Union Pacific Railroad.*

] 22 [
DARK ISLAND CASTLE–
THE TOWERS

DARK ISLAND CASTLE, CENTRALLY LOCATED IN THE Thousand Islands area of the St. Lawrence Seaway, opposite Chippewa Bay, New York, was constructed by former Singer Sewing Machine president, Frederick G. Bourne. Bourne had promised his family a summer retreat on the seven-acre island that commands a wonderful view both up and down the great St. Lawrence River. His "shooting and fishing shack," as he called it, was to be a surprise for his family and no doubt it was, because the structure turned out to be a twenty-eight-room towered castle with several rooms over thirty feet in length and fifteen feet high. The Towers, so named by Bourne, was designed by architect Ernest Flagg, who also built the Singer Building, one of the first skyscrapers in New York City.

The castellated, stone structure was erected between 1904 and 1906, using granite quarried at Oak Island and transported by boat to the construction site. The castle was built into ledge rock on the island's small hill overlooking the irregular, rocky shoreline below. The basic design of The Towers is similar to Scottish-style castle architecture but features a Spanish, red-tile roof with towers, turrets, and battlemented wall perimeters. Though the main structure is three stories high above ground level, portions of the castle extend above the roof, giving it a much higher appearance on its hilltop site.

The twenty-eight rooms with oak floors include seventeen spacious bedrooms and eleven modern baths with built-in tubs and stall showers. The ground floor entrance hall, with its stone, arched walls and ceilings, measures thirty-six by thirty-three feet with five-foot-wide stone steps leading up to the main floor. Other rooms on the ground floor are the large thirty-two-by-eighteen-foot library, five bedrooms, four baths, servants' sitting and dining rooms, and two kitchens with built-in refrigerator and dumbwaiter.

The main floor contains a thirty-seven-by-thirty-foot auditorium with several windows on each of three walls. The living room is a large chamber measuring thirty-six feet square and containing a huge, pink, marble fireplace. This magnificent room also features three pullman window seats and two very large, tile-floored sun-porches, one containing a great, stone fireplace. The thirty-by-twenty-foot dining room has high, oak-paneled walls contrasting a beautiful marble fireplace. The dining room is serviced from the butler's pantry and a serving room with dumbwaiter service from the kitchens below.

The upper floor is occupied by several bedrooms, many over twenty feet in length with connecting baths, one of which is circular. A large massage room is also located on this floor.

On one portion of the building is the top floor,

with a thirty-by-twenty-two-foot dormitory and bath, and an additional large bedroom with bath. The tower room is sixteen feet square and contains its own fireplace.

The basement has additional servants' quarters of three bedrooms and a bath. Storerooms and laundry are also located here. The basement's furnace room has the necessary facilities that supply oil steam heat serviced by a five-thousand-gallon fuel-oil storage tank. Other utilities include a diesel electric plant and two pumps supplying river water for household use. Drinking water is brought in separately from the mainland.

Several other notable buildings were also constructed on this island paradise, one of which is a five-story clock tower about fifteen feet square, built close to the castle with an enclosed corridor providing direct access from the castle to the upper floor of the tower. The clock tower has twelve-foot-diameter clock faces with six-foot hands on each of its upper four sides. This tower is also attached to the smaller of the two large boathouses on the islands.

Bourne was commodore of the New York Yacht Club for many years and owned several small boats in addition to a beautiful steam yacht. Decks and boat servicing facilities were constructed to accommodate these boats, which were frequently seen cruising among the Thousand Islands waters. An elaborate, stone boathouse with a slip 18 by 125 feet was built for the one-hundred-foot steam yacht. This boathouse also contained quarters with nine bedrooms and two baths in addition to a generator room, battery room, water and fire pumps, and screw jacks to raise the yacht from the water for winter storage. A 15-by-250-foot dock bordered the boathouse with its numerous windows and crenellated roof perimeter.

The smaller boathouse, adjoining the clock tower, is one hundred feet in length and was used to accommodate the fleet of smaller boats. The walls are a series of enclosed, broad arches with a tiled roof similar to that of the castle building.

Other structures on the island are a squash court building with its twenty-five-by-fifty-four-foot maple-lined court, and eighteen-by-sixty-five-foot brick-paved pavilion that overlooks a large lawn-tennis court. A twelve-foot brick wall circles from the landing to the castle entrance with several footpaths winding through the island's woodlands of evergreens, poplars, and other fine old trees. High, stone retaining walls near the smaller boathouse blend well with the stone of the upper level walls and surrounding buildings.

Covered passages were built from the docks to the castle as a protection during stormy weather. Heavy seas tempered by high winds sometimes make passage to the mainland practically impossible. But the buildings are well constructed and self-sufficient with elaborate heating and lighting facilities.

Commodore Bourne spent many happy years on the island with his family, enjoying its vacation luxury and entertaining prominent guests. When Bourne died in March, 1919, he left the Dark Island Castle to his daughter, Mrs. Alexander D. Thayer. In 1928 Mr. and Mrs. Thayer made additions to the castle, which they occupied for several years. The La Salle Military Academy of Oakdale, Long Island, New York, also used The Towers as a summer extension, and upon the death of Mrs. Thayer in May, 1962, the Dark Island property was given as a bequest to the academy. Because of the distance of the estate, the property was later sold in 1965 to become a children's camp operated by the Christian Houses for Children, Incorporated, an organization in existence since 1930. Today the Dark Island Castle still stands and is privately owned.

The island was known in early days by the Indians who called it Lone Star, later to be named Dark Island when charts of the waterway were published. Early use of the island by Indians is validated by the numbers of arrowheads and other Indian artifacts that were discovered on the island. The castle with its cluster of other attractive buildings was once opened a number of times to public tours and has been an admired landmark of the St. Lawrence River area since its construction.

Dark Island Castle showing the main building, clock tower, and one of the boat houses. The castle was named "The Towers" by its owner, Mr. Frederick G. Bourne. *Courtesy St. Lawrence County History Center.*

Close-up view of the Dark Island Castle main building. *Courtesy St. Lawrence County History Center.*

Dark Island Castle and small boathouse. *Courtesy Previews, Inc.*

The large boathouse of Dark Island Castle. *Courtesy Previews, Inc.*

Entrance hall of The Towers with armor display. *Courtesy Previews, Inc.*

Castle entrance doors. *Courtesy Previews, Inc.*

A portion of the clock tower. *Courtesy Prieviews, Inc.*

] 23 [

NEMACOLIN CASTLE

NEMACOLIN CASTLE, ALSO KNOWN AS BOWMAN Castle and Nemacolin Towers, is located in historic Brownsville near the Monongahela River, thirty-six miles south of Pittsburgh, Pennsylvania. The castle was constructed in 1789 by Jacob Bowman, a pioneer who migrated from Hagenstown, Maryland, settling in Brownsville in February of 1786.

The site of the castle had once been occupied by Redstone Old Fort, also known as Fort Burd, built by Colonel James Burd for the British and visited by many Indian traders and hunters in its day. Previous to building the castle, Bowman had erected a log dwelling on the site, which Fayette County deeds show he purchased in the summer of 1788 at a cost of twenty-three pounds. This log dwelling was used as a trading post that Bowman called Nemacolin, after a famous Indian chief who had once lived on the property. The fort and the trading post existed for several years as an important stopping-off point for western immigration and trips down the Monongahela River.

With many settlers waiting to travel west, the trading post soon became a thriving business, and it was eventually incorporated as a room in the castle during its construction. The castle is built of brick, primarily on two floors with a three-story, octagonal tower to the left of the main entrance, and a square, third-story tower room at the rear of the building opposite the octagonal tower. The castle has twenty-two rooms, with battlements, balconies, bay windows, high-arched porches, and roofs varying in elevation and design.

The battlemented, octagonal tower rises one story above the two-story principal building with windows located in alternate locations on its three floors. Four arched windows are on the upper tower floor, with rectangular windows on the floors below all having louvered shutters, as do numerous other windows throughout the castle. A small balcony on the tower's second floor level has balustrades and a heavy railing similar in design to the other balconies on this facade.

Adjoining this tower is the centrally located main entrance, above which is an arcaded balcony that provides an excellent view of the valley and river for some distance. A series of battlements span the roof perimeter of this central portion of the castle that joins a two-story wing perpendicular to it. This wing is of higher elevation than the rest of the castle, except for the towers, and gives evidence of the 15-foot-high ceilings within some of its rooms. Like its lower, adjoining, two-story portion of the castle, the roof of this higher wing is pitched with a noticeable roof overhang surrounding it, not found elsewhere on the castle. The large bay window of this wing, to the right of the main entrance, is a projection of the first floor with a balcony occupying the roof space above this window.

The square, third-story tower room on the rear of the lower building portions has a low-pitched, pyramidal roof with narrow, twin, arched windows on its walls. Below this tower room extension, on the second floor, is an oriel window with a tiny balcony projecting to its immediate left from the exterior wall. High, latticed woodwork, designed in a series of arches, rises to the roof extension of an open porch to the right of the rear tower room. The windows of the castle are generally rectangular in their framing with a variation in dimensions.

Within many of the castle's spacious rooms are glass chandeliers and a variety of fireplaces differing in design and materials. All brick and stone fireplaces contrast to those of arched marble, and beautiful carved oak mantels supported by twin corbels and colonnette as in the sitting room. The library contains an extensive collection numbering several thousand books and magazines, some of which are first editions that belonged to the Bowman family.

Several of the rooms contain fine, mahogany furniture that blends well with the rooms. Some imported furnishings include three grandfather clocks, each eight feet in height, which were brought from England, and two four-foot-high Carrara marble statues, one a replica of the Marble Faun, the other of a Grecian figure, brought from Venice, Italy. Tapestries and other fine antiques are also found in the various rooms.

In the high-ceilinged hallway a circular staircase leads to the second floor, which is occupied by several spacious bedrooms, many with beautiful, large, Louis XV four-poster beds. Other items of interest in the bedrooms are the heavy marble washstand, pitchers, basins, and other toilet articles and other pieces of fine furniture.

Modern facilities added to the castle include plumbing, electric lighting, refrigeration, and furnace heating facilities. Ornate gas lamps outside the castle have electric lights, but still maintain their old-time charm and character. The castle gardens have walks and several large shade trees whose great spreading branches add to the Old-World atmosphere of the place. Other structures on the property include a greenhouse and stables.

Bowman was an active person during his lifetime. In 1794 he was commissary to government troops during the Whiskey Rebellion, and in 1795 he was commissioned as a justice of the peace. Also in 1795 Bowman was appointed by President George Washington as Brownsville's first postmaster, a position he held for thirty-four years until 1829. Bowman founded the Monongahela Bank in 1814, and was its president until 1843 when he retired. His other activities included the building of machinery and construction of boats.

Some notable persons who visited Brownsville were General Lafayette, who was given an enthusiastic reception there in 1811, and General Andrew Jackson, who was also warmly received by the inhabitants in 1837. Bowman was very well known over all of western Pennsylvania as a community leader until his death in 1847.

The Nemacolin Castle remained in the Bowman family for many years. The castle, now operated and maintained by the Brownsville Historical Society, exists today as a reminder of America's early pioneer days when many buckskin-clad settlers stopped there before heading to the dark, unknown West.

Nemacolin Castle, built in 1789 by Jacob Bowman, is
still standing in Brownsville, Pennsylvania. The castle
has 22 rooms with towers, turrets, and battlements.
Courtesy Brownsville Historical Society.

Rear View of the castle displays an oriel window and square tower. Old-time lamps on the grounds are now fixed with electric lighting. *Courtesy West Penn Power Company.*

Interior room of Nemacolin Castle displaying interesting fireplace and antiques. *Courtesy West Penn Power Company.*

] 24 [

CARMELITE MONASTERY

IN 1790 A GROUP OF CARMELITE NUNS, AN AN-cient religious order that originated on Mount Carmel in Palestine, journeyed to America, settling in Baltimore, Maryland, where they established their first home in the New World. Since that time branches of the Carmelite order spread to other states, where foundations of the Carmelites were settled in monasteries.

It was in 1932 that a small group of sisters were transferred to Indianapolis, Indiana, to occupy the first completed wing of their new castellated monastery. Located on an eighteen-acre tract of land, the monastery, begun in 1929 and dedicated in October 1932, is reminiscent of the walls and towers of medieval European castles, particularly those of the Spanish town of Ávila.

The main building structure, with its adjoining battlemented towers, encloses a large, inner courtyard, bordered partially by cloistered walkways and gardens. The outer perimeter of the monastery is constructed of flat brownstone of various sizes blended in a rugged, pleasing design. The roof line of the exterior front walls is uniformly battlemented, as are the main towers. Arched windows are set deep in the stone walls with sloping, stone sills protruding from many of the upper windows. Sloping, stone slabs also extend slightly from their position between the broad merlons of the wall and tower battlements.

The south corner of the structure is occupied by four lofty, battlemented towers, each separated from the other by high portions of the building walls. The lower halves of these towers gradually increase in size with their bases having greater diameters than their upper portions. A large niche, built into the front wall between two of the towers, contains a sculptured statue of Saint Teresa of Ávila, who founded the Reform of Carmel in 1562.

The massive front portals contain large, heavy, recessed doors, both set within stone, arched, alcoved entranceways. The north entry is located within a protruding, rectangular vestibule with two large, twin towers on opposite exterior side walls. These towers are of similar design and size to the four great south towers.

The other front entrance is centrally located between the south and north towers. This semicircular, protruding entranceway increases in diameter at its base in a similar manner to the main towers. Pairs of high, narrow windows, spaced by a small column mullion, flank the arched, stone-alcoved entrance. Both entrances have paired columns supporting decorative, carved arches, above which is found the seal of the order faced on the stone wall.

The public entry leads to a vestibule that gives access to a long, vaulted-ceilinged lobby with a stone floor. Adjoining the lobby is the high-ceilinged outer turn room, so named because of the turntable parcel receiver located within a partitioned wall of the room and adjoining chamber. A larger visitors room, entered from a corridor, contains a large grill that permits partitioned communication with visitors.

Numerous corridors and rooms of various dimensions and designs are found throughout this holy sanctuary with its silent atmosphere and Old-World charm. Among the monastery's many rooms are the choirroom, vestments room, refectory, baking room, and sleeping chambers or cells of the twenty-one sisters who occupy the building.

Behind the two north towers, a new wing of contemporary design was completed in 1961. A new chapel was also erected, replacing the old, smaller chapel formally located in one of the north towers. Much of the finishing work on the new wing was done by the sisters, whose skill also led them to design and fabricate recessed Holy Water fonts within the chapel. Included in the new wing are the chapters room, infirmary rooms, pharmacy, recreation room, and nun's choir room with its sliding doors that open to the chapel but that are separated by a large, screened grate. The sisters are expert seamstresses, making beautiful vestments and altar cloths in their new sewing center.

Within the older portions of the monastery, columned openings of the inner court cloisters are spanned by high, brick arches whose ends rest on varied-designed capitals of circular columns. Square, stone columns support arches of cloisters at the open, north courtyard.

Pleasant, winding pathways, small, stone-lined ponds, rock gardens, and numerous trees and shrubs make up the beautiful landscaping of the monastery grounds. Various shrines combined with the picturesque gardens offer a place of solitude and prayer within the monastery walls.

The Carmelite nuns follow a chosen rigorous life that is dedicated to prayer, self-denial, poverty, manual labor, and silence most of their long day. But this is done in a spirit of joy, a united application and devotion unchanged with the passage of time.

Despite the contemporary addition to the monastery, there still remains the ageless beauty of medieval architecture. The lofty circular towers and rugged stone of the battlemented walls are now caressed by the spreading fingers of ivy that add to the charm and serenity of the Carmelite monastery.

The ivy-covered walls of Carmelite Monastery located in Indianapolis, Indiana. Construction of the monastery was begun in 1929 and dedicated in 1932. *Courtesy Sisters of the Carmelite Monastery.*

The Carmelite Monastery is reminiscent of European castles, especially of the Spanish town of Avila. *Courtesy Sisters of the Carmelite Monastery.*

One of the entryways with arched windows typical of this facade. *Photo by Robert Lavelle, courtesy Sisters of the Carmelite Monastery.*

] 25 [

GREY TOWERS CASTLE

ONE OF THE MOST ARCHITECTURALLY SIGNIFICANT castles in the United States is Grey Towers Castle, located at Glenside, Pennsylvania, a suburb of the city of Philadelphia. The castle was built by William Welsh Harrison, a retired sugar refiner, who in 1881 purchased the extensive country estate of J. Thomas Audenried that lay in the vicinity of the historic Harmer Hill village.

In 1882 after the existing mansion on the property was destroyed by fire, Harrison decided to build Grey Towers Castle. Philadelphia architect Horace Trumbauer designed the massive structure, following the architecture of the great, twelfth-century Alnwick Castle in England.

During the long ten years of constructing the many-turreted and battlemented castle, the Harrisons took residence in the elaborate gatehouse on the property. Other buildings on the estate included a power-plant, a large building for servants' quarters, a stately carriage house, stables, an elaborate conservatory, and arboretums.

In 1892 the grey, hand-dressed stone castle was completed with overall dimensions of 225 by 185 feet. The numerous circular towers located at several corners of the castle vary in height, all containing deep rectangular and arched casemented windows. Battlements uniformly encircle the towers and principal roof perimeters in addition to the smaller turrets projecting above the main towers. A light, contrasting, cement trim is used over the entire exterior of the castle, highlighting the battlements, window casements, balconies, entries, and broad arches of the massive entry portico. A similar light-color concrete mixture is used in the extensive and elaborate exterior double stairways and balustrades. The castle exterior is further adorned with sculptures of grotesques, griffins, and gargoyles at various walls and towers.

Imported building materials were used for the forty-one interior rooms of the castle. Exquisite fresco ceilings are found in several rooms of the main floor, with ceilings of the drawing room and ballroom painted by a European artist, the latter being done in France and then transported to the castle. In addition to the beautiful ballroom and drawing room, other principal rooms include a dining room, lobby, library, and billiard room located under the main stairway and now used as an apartment. Tower rooms located at corners of the castle are now used as study areas on the second and third floors. Stained and Belgian cut glass are used in an appealing display in the deep, casemented window frames. The former dining room and office to the right of the main entrance are finished in oak with ornamented, carved trim in the panels. The library to the left of this entrance is now used as an office.

The large castle lobby, with its grand staircase and surrounding upper balcony, is finished in wood with mahogany floors inlaid without the use of nails. Solid mahogany is also used in the staircase, spindles, and balcony. A variety of beautifully designed and highly ornate lighting fixtures flank the staircase, ceiling, and sides of the upper projecting balcony floors. The lobby side walls each have large, marble fireplaces with mantels of carved Italian marble. Broad, shallow arches are found on both the first-floor lobby and upper balcony level with paired, double columns and detailed capitals. Beautiful, ornate chandeliers, fine tapestries, Mexican onyx bath fixtures, and other such notable features are found throughout this majestic castle.

In 1928 the William Welsh Harrison estate was purchased and transformed to become the new, fifty-five-acre site of Beaver College, a liberal arts college for women. Grey Towers Castle now serves as dormitory and social center of this fine educational institution. It is interesting to note that Alnwick Castle in England has also become a women's college, known as Alnwick Training College.

Grey Towers Castle remains in the excellent condition in which it was when first constructed. The lofty, battlemented castle is a prominent landmark and visual reminder, reminiscent of those far-off medieval times of armor-suited men and horses that once passed through their castle gates.

Grey Towers Castle at Glenside, Pennsylvania, was designed after the twelfth-century Alnwick Castle in England. The castle has numerous towers and battlements, and is now used as a dormitory for girls as part of Beaver College. *Photo by Harry J. Utzy, courtesy Beaver College.*

Detail of terrace stairs and tower showing the beautiful architecture of the castle. *Photo by Harry Utzy, courtesy Beaver College.*

Massive portico of Grey Towers Castle. The expert masonry is typical of this castle. *Photo by Harry J. Utzy, courtesy Beaver College.*